ADVAITA VEDĀNTA: A PHILOSOPHICAL RECONSTRUCTION

Advaita Vedānta:

A PHILOSOPHICAL RECONSTRUCTION

by Eliot Deutsch

EAST-WEST CENTER PRESS
HONOLULU

By Eliot Deutsch

The Bhagavad Gītā (New York, 1968)

Advaita Vedānta: A Philosophical Reconstruction (Honolulu, 1969)

Standard Book Number 8248-0085-0
Library of Congress Catalog Card Number 69-19282
Printed in the United States of America
First Edition

Preface

"Comparative Philosophy" means many things to different scholars and thinkers. To some it means an exploration of non-Western philosophies (and religions) in order to find, to accept, or to assimilate those values, ideas, and concerns that one believes to be missing in one's own culture; to others it means an objective, scholarly examination of various individual thinkers and schools of Asian philosophy, and sometimes the comparing and contrasting of these with leading Western examples, in order to promote greater knowledge and understanding of the East; and still to others it means an articulation of the basic "ways of thinking" which are exhibited as persistent cultural traits in various civilizations both for the sake of knowledge and for a possible synthesis of Western and Eastern philosophy. Through the immense efforts of many workers in all these areas of comparative philosophy Westerners, with an interest in Asia, have come to an understanding of the patterns and structures of thought in Asian cultures, of the history of various traditions in the East, and of the intricacies and subtleties of specific systems and individuals in these traditions. A great deal of work still remains to be done in all these areas, and indeed an enormous amount of significant research in comparative philosophy is being carried out today by both Western and Eastern scholars.

But it is also becoming increasingly apparent that we are ready to pursue new goals in comparative philosophy and to bring comparative philosophy into the mainstream of *creative* thought—East and West. We are aware now that there is much of intrinsic philosophical value and interest in Asian thought and that consequently this thought need not be cast merely in the mold of an historical (or exotic) curiosity. Students ought to be able to study

Asian philosophy simply for the purpose of enriching their philosophical background and enabling them to deal better with the philosophical problems that interest them. Without losing sight of the distinctive and sometimes unique characteristics of a tradition one ought to be able to concentrate on a tradition as it is a response to a series of universal questions and problems, and with the express intention that these responses will influence one spontaneously in one's own thinking. A new goal for comparative philosophy, in short, would be to approach Asian philosophy as material for creative thought. I am quite convinced that on its merit Asian philosophy is indeed worthy of being approached in this spirit. This little book is but one small effort pointing in the direction of that goal.

I wish to thank the American Institute of Indian Studies for enabling me to spend a year in India (1963–64) to pursue further research in Advaita Vedānta. Without the opportunity for study and discussion afforded by that experience this work would not have been possible. I also wish to thank the University of Hawaii for making it possible for me to return to India for some weeks in 1967 to attend the Indian Philosophical Congress meetings in Benares and to meet again with Indian colleagues. I am grateful to the publishers of *International Philosophical Quarterly*, *Philosophy East and West*, and *Darshana International* for permission to use a substantial part of materials for Chapters II, IV, and V, which originally appeared in those publications. Material in Chapter III was presented as a paper at the University Seminar in Oriental Philosophy and Religion at Columbia University in April, 1965 and I am grateful to the participants in this faculty seminar for their stimulating and searching questions.

Honolulu, Hawaii
December, 1968

Contents

TO SANNA

ADVAITA VEDĀNTA: A PHILOSOPHICAL RECONSTRUCTION

Introduction

The term "Vedānta" literally means "end of the Veda" and refers, within the Indian philosophical tradition, to the teachings of the Upaniṣads, the *Brahma-sūtras*, and the *Bhagavadgītā* and to the various philosophical systematizations of them.[1] Advaita Vedānta is the non-dualistic system of Vedānta expounded primarily by Śaṁkara (*ca.* 788–820). It has been, and continues to be, the most widely accepted system of thought among philosophers in India, and it is, we believe, one of the greatest philosophical achievements to be found in the East or the West.[2]

1 These three works (or collections of works) are known as the *prasthānas* or "foundations" of systematic Vedānta. All the schools of Vedānta—e.g., Rāmānuja's Viśiṣṭādvaita ("qualified non-dualism") and Madhva's Dvaita ("dualism")—recognize them as authoritative. In referring to these works, we will draw most heavily from the early Upaniṣads and the *Brahma-sūtras*, with its classical commentaries. The *Bhagavadgītā* is not, for Advaita Vedānta, as important as these other works, and for the very good reason that the *Gītā* is not primarily an Advaitic treatise. It does, to be sure, contain an Advaitic dimension, but on the whole it presents a more pronounced theistic orientation. (Cf. the author's *Bhagavad Gītā* [New York: Holt, Rinehart and Winston, Inc., 1968] and Edgerton's and S. Radhakrishnan's translations and introductory essays on the *Gītā*.)

2 Śaṁkara's system is best labeled "non-dualistic" rather than "monistic" to distinguish it from any position that views reality as a single order of *objective* being. Advaita Vedānta is concerned to show the ultimate non-reality of all distinctions—that Reality is not constituted by parts, that in essence it is not-different from the Self. The unity or "oneness" that Advaita upholds, as we will see later in close detail, does not require variety or multiplicity, as in the case with most monistic views, in order to be affirmed.

Advaita Vedānta was developed further by many followers of Śaṁkara over a period of several hundred years. Thinkers such as Sureśvara (ninth century), Maṇḍana (ninth century), Padmapāda (ninth century), Sarvajñātman (tenth century), Vācaspati Miśra (tenth century), Śrī Harṣa (twelfth century), Prakāśātman (thirteenth century),

At the same time, Advaita Vedānta is more than a philosophical system, as we understand these terms in the West today; it is also a practical guide to spiritual experience, and is intimately bound up with spiritual experience. The Advaitin is convinced that "to know" is "to be"; that one acquires knowledge only in an act of conscious being which is akin to what one knows and is the content of direct experience. "Disease," Śaṁkara notes, "is not cured by pronouncing 'medicine,' but by taking it."[3] Advaita Vedānta is a religion as much as it is a technical philosophy; it is a way of spiritual realization as well as a system of thought.

This intimacy between religion and philosophy in Advaita Vedānta, as in much of the Indian tradition, has been pointed out frequently. It bears constant repetition, however, for there are still a few philosophers who, in their desire to find a dominant naturalistic tradition in India, are determined to neglect (or even to deny) this relationship. At the same time, one must be careful to guard against a kind of non-thinking sentimental piety which would have us believe that Vedānta is pure and simple religion—that everything about it is "sacred," "holy," "true," and "morally uplifting" and is thus immune to rational criticism. As this work will attempt to show, there is a great deal of rigorous thought in Vedānta which is not simply superadded to its religious aspects. Vedānta's concern

Vidyāraṇya (fourteenth century), Prakāśānanda (sixteenth century), Sadānanda (sixteenth century), Appaya Dīkṣita (sixteenth century), and Dharmarāja (seventeenth century) made many valuable contributions to the main doctrines in Śaṁkara's works. Further, Śaṁkara himself acknowledges his indebtedness to earlier Advaitic thinkers, namely, Gauḍapāda (seventh? century), the teacher of his teacher Govinda. We will in the course of this work make many references to post-Śaṁkara Advaitins; the main body of doctrine associated with systematic Advaita, however, will be drawn from Śaṁkara. As formulated by him, the system stands in its most pristine state, not being overburdened, as is often the case later on, by scholastic subtleties and dialectical controversies.

3 Śaṁkara, *Viveka-cūḍāmaṇi*, vs. 64. Translations of all Sanskrit passages quoted are mine unless otherwise indicated.

with spiritual realization, in short, does not make it less of a technical philosophy.

One of the major difficulties that we in the West have with Indian thought in general, and with Vedānta in particular, nevertheless, is to be found in what may be called its "traditional grounding." A Vedāntic system bases itself upon ancient texts, and one of its primary tasks is to show that these texts represent a consistent (and singular) viewpoint. Systematic Vedāntic was thus formulated in terms of scriptural exegesis as much as it was formulated in terms of philosophical analysis. The exegetical dimension of Vedānta is of great interest to students of linguistics and Indian cultural history (and naturally to Indian scholars themselves), but it is of very little interest to Western students of philosophy. We do not accept the authority of the Veda (or, for the most part, the authority of any other scripture); consequently, we are not concerned whether one system or another best interprets certain obscure passages in it. Our criterion of philosophical truth or significance is not whether a particular system of thought is consistent with some other body of work; rather, it is whether that system of thought is "consistent" with human experience. Philosophically, we judge a system of thought in terms of its adequacy in organizing the various dimensions of our experience; in terms of its providing us with new ways of looking at, of gaining insight into, the nature of the world and of our life in it; and in terms of the kinds of arguments used to sustain these insights. Further, most of us who are acquainted with the ancient Indian religious-philosophical texts are quite convinced that they do not express a single, consistent viewpoint, but that they express a very rich diversity of experience and reflection upon it.[4]

4 This is readily apparent in the Upaniṣads alone, which were undoubtedly set down over a period of several hundred years. The early Upaniṣads (e.g., *Bṛhad-āraṇyaka, Chāndogya*) lend themselves more easily to an Advaitic interpretation than do some of the later ones (e.g., *Īśā, Śvetāśvatara*).

In reconstructing Advaita Vedānta, we intend to focus on philosophical analysis at the expense of scriptural exegesis. We want to find in Advaita Vedānta that which is philosophically meaningful to a Westerner and to articulate this content in universal philosophical terms. A reconstruction need not be, nor should it be, a distortion (or a mere modernizing) of the system. Although specific doctrines may be modified, in the sense of making explicit what is merely implicit in them, and although much that is of mere historical interest may be neglected, the real philosophical content and vision of the original system must indeed be retained. What emerges from a reconstruction of a Vedāntic system is also not itself another Vedāntic system; for by neglecting the arguments used to interpret scripture and to force it into a consistent mold, one removes the possibility of making such a claim.

A reconstruction of Advaita Vedānta is an attempt to formulate systematically one's understanding of what is of universal philosophical interest in it. To do this, one must necessarily distill from an enormous body of literature only that which is of immediate value to one's task and present it, not so much through comparisons with other Indian or Western systems of thought, but in its own dynamic terms. Systematic Advaita Vedānta was developed in a dialectical context with other Vedāntic and especially non-Vedāntic Indian systems and thinkers (e.g., the Nyāya, Sāṁkhya, Yoga; the Buddhists, the Jains). Therefore, to understand it in the cultural-historical sense, one cannot neglect this context. A reconstruction, however, is not strictly a work of scholarship. It is not an attempt to work out similarities and differences between two or more systems; nor is it primarily an attempt to exposit and interpret the main thoughts or specific arguments of a philosophical school for its own sake. In a reconstruction, exposition and interpretation must certainly be present, but it is not necessary that the system that is to be reconstructed, in this case Advaita Vedānta, be treated as a "historical" school. What is necessary is that we look only for that which is still philosophically alive within the system and deal with it accordingly.

The reconstruction of Advaita Vedānta that we propose to undertake, therefore, is a re-creative presentation of an Eastern philosophy in which the philosophy is lifted somewhat out of its historical and traditional context and is treated as a system of thought and path of spiritual experience capable of being understood by any student of philosophy.

1 Brahman

There is a principle of utter simplicity ubiquitous in Nature. The wise realize it as silence divine.

Brahman, the One, is a state of being. It is not a "He," a personal being; nor is it an "It," an impersonal concept. Brahman is that state which *is* when all subject/object distinctions are obliterated. Brahman is ultimately a name for the experience of the timeless plenitude of being.[1]

I

Brahman is designated by Advaitins as *saccidānanda*: as "being" (*sat*), "consciousness" (*cit*), and "bliss" (*ānanda*). These are not so much qualifying attributes of Brahman as they are the terms that express the apprehension of Brahman by man. *Saccidānanda* is a symbol of Brahman as formulated by the mind interpreting its Brahman-experience.[2]

1 The term "Brahman" first appears in the *Ṛg Veda* (*ca.* 1200 B.C.) in close connection with various sacred utterances that were thought to have a special magical power. Originally, then, the term may have meant "spell" or "prayer"; an utterance that was used for the magical attainment of worldly wishes and other worldly desires. Later, in the Brāhmaṇas, Brahman comes to signify that which stands behind the gods as their ground and source, and in the Upaniṣads generally it becomes the unitary principle of all being, the knowledge of which liberates one from finitude.

2 Advaitic thinkers refer to this type of designation as "definition with reference to essence" (*svarūpalakṣaṇa*) as distinguished from a "definition with reference to accidents" (*taṭasthalakṣaṇa*). With the designation of Brahman as *saccidānanda*, we have an essential identification of *sat, cit, ānanda* with Brahman rather than an adjectival qualifying of Brahman. In other words, *sat, cit, ānanda* are not intended to be qualifying attributes or accidents of Brahman, i.e., something that is superadded to it; they are intended to be expressions of its essence. Our

Being (*sat*)—apart from its complex historical-linguistic associations—points to the ontological principle of unity,[3] to the oneness not constituted of parts, to the existential substratum of all subjects and objects. Brahman is experienced as pure unqualified being. In fact it alone truly "exists"—which is to say that its manner of being is not comparable to the supposed existence of anything else. Consciousness (*cit*) points to the principle of awareness which informs being and which is, for the Advaitin, an unchanging witness of our being. Brahman-experience is illuminating experience; it is a state of conscious enlightenment. And it is a state of joyous being. Bliss (*ānanda*) points to the principle of value; to the fact that Brahman-experience is ecstatic and annuls all partial value in its incomparable splendor.

Phenomenologically, then, Brahman is affirmed by the Advaitin as that fullness of being which enlightens and is joy. It has its basis for him in experience (*anubhava*), not in mere speculation; and the experience, which is enduring for one who attains it, is the goal of human life.

II

And yet Brahman is not *saccidānanda*, if by that designation a positive limiting character is given to Brahman. Brahman, as transcendental being given in spiritual experience, defies all description or characterization. As Yājñavalkya, the Upaniṣadic sage, holds: "There is no other or better description [of Brahman] than

main contention here, though, is that these terms are really being used properly not so much in a logical as in a phenomenological manner, for the problem is not so much one of defining Brahman as it is one of describing the fundamental features of man's experience of Oneness.

3 Cf. J. A. B. van Buitenen's Introduction to *Rāmānuja's Vedārthasaṃgraha* ("Deccan College Monograph Series," 16 [Poona: 1956]) for an excellent discussion of the historical-philosophical development of *sat*.

this; that it is not-this, not-this (*neti neti*)."[4] And as Śaṁkara notes regarding the definition of Brahman—*satyaṁ jñānam anantam brahma*, Brahman is truth, knowledge, infinite—words like *satya* (truth, reality) serve to "differentiate Brahman from other entities that possess opposite qualities."[5] Experientially, the role of a positive characterization or definition of Brahman is to direct the mind towards Brahman by affirming essential qualities that are really only denials of their opposites. To say "Brahman is truth" negates the quality of untruth—and this negation, it is believed, serves pragmatically to orient the mind towards Brahman. All characterizations of Brahman, in short, are intended in their experiential dimension to aid those who are searching for Brahman but have not yet realized It.

The *via negativa* of Advaita Vedānta also safeguards the unqualified oneness of that state of being called Brahman and silences all argument that would seek either to demonstrate or to refute it. Human language has its source in phenomenal experience; hence, it is limited in its application to states of being that are beyond that experience; logic is grounded in the mind as it relates to the phenomenal order; hence, it is unable to affirm, without at the same time denying, what extends beyond that order. "All determination is negation"; to apply a predicate to something is to impose a limitation upon it; for, logically, something is being excluded from the subject. The Real is without internal difference and, in essence, is unrelated to the content of any other form of experience. The Real is thus unthinkable: thought can be brought to it only through negations of what is thinkable.[6]

4 *Bṛhad-āranyaka Upaniṣad*, II, 3, 6.
5 Śaṁkara's Commentary on *Taittirīya Upaniṣad*, II, 1, 1.
6 Cf. Śaṁkara, *Brahmasūtrabhāṣya*, II, 1, 6; II, 1, 11; also his Commentary on *Bṛhad-āraṇyaka Upaniṣad*, I, 4, 6. Advaitins have, nevertheless, proffered arguments, if not "rational proofs," for Brahman. These arguments, as we have suggested, function primarily in a pragmatic con-

Advaita Vedānta, then, must labor under this fact, which it explicitly acknowledges, that whatever is expressed is ultimately non-Brahman, is ultimately untrue.

III

Advaita Vedānta thus distinguishes two aspects or modes of Brahman, *nirguṇa* and *saguṇa*. *Nirguṇa* Brahman—Brahman without qualities—is just that transcendent indeterminate state of being about which ultimately nothing can be affirmed. *Saguṇa* Brahman—Brahman with qualities—is Brahman as interpreted and affirmed by the mind from its necessarily limited standpoint; it is that about which something can be said. And it is also a kind of spiritual experience.[7]

text of orienting the mind towards the possibility of Brahman-experience. The most common Advaitic argument for Brahman has to do with "necessary existence." Reminiscent of (but differing in many interesting and obvious ways from) Thomas' "third proof," the Advaitin argues that there must be a ground or substratum to experience, for otherwise it would be impossible to deny or negate the existence of anything. Śaṁkara puts it this way: "Whenever we deny something unreal, we do so with reference to something real; the unreal snake, e.g. is negatived with reference to the real rope. But this (denial of something unreal with reference to something real) is possible only if some entity is left. If everything is denied, no entity is left, and if no entity is left, the denial of some other which we may wish to undertake, becomes impossible, i.e. that latter entity becomes real and as such cannot be negatived."—*Brahmasūtrabhāṣya*, III, 2, 22, in *The Vedānta-Sūtras with the Commentary of Śaṅkarācārya*, trans. by George Thibaut, Vols. XXXIV and XXXVIII of *Sacred Books of the East*, ed. by Max Müller (Oxford: The Clarendon Press, 1890 and 1896).

This argument will be clearer from the discussion in the next chapter, which provides the ontological distinctions and psychological processes that are presupposed in the argument.

7 This interpretation of *saguṇa* Brahman—as a type of spiritual experience as well as an epistemic transformation of *nirguṇa* Brahman into an object—is justified, we believe, on the grounds that Śaṁkara and other Advaitins insist that *saguṇa* Brahman (also referred to in this type of context as Īśvara, the Lord) is a proper object of devotion and, when

Brahman is a state of silent being; it is also a dynamic becoming. Brahman is divine and the Divine is Brahman.

This divine status of Brahman is not to be construed, however, in this context, as a personal deity who responds to prayer, bestows grace, or enters into history; rather, like *nirguṇa* Brahman, *saguṇa* Brahman is a state of being. It is a state of being wherein all distinctions between subject and object are harmonized. In *nirguṇa* Brahman all distinctions are obliterated and are overcome; in *saguṇa* Brahman they are integrated: a duality in unity is present here, and, consequently, the power of love. *Nirguṇa* Brahman is a state of mental-spiritual enlightenment (*jñāna*); *saguṇa* Brahman is a state of vital loving awareness (*bhakti*). *Nirguṇa* Brahman is conceptually an objectification of spiritual experience without distinction or determination (*nirvikalpa samādhi*); *saguṇa* Brahman is an objectification of determinate spiritual experience (*savikalpa samādhi*). It is the experience that, although negated by *nirguṇa* Brahman, yet complements *nirguṇa* Brahman-experience and, because it takes up and harmonizes everything within itself, makes possible the affirmation of the spirituality or intrinsic value of all modes of being.

In sum: Brahman, for Advaita Vedānta, is a name for that fullness of being which is the "content" of non-dualistic spiritual experience: an experience in which all distinctions between subject and object are shattered and in which remains only a pure, unqualified "oneness." The characterization of Brahman as *saccidānanda*—as infinite being (*sat*), consciousness (*cit*), and bliss (*ānanda*)—is intended not so much to ascribe attributes to Brahman as it is to describe the primary moments or features of the non-dualistic

realized in experience, is a state of loving bliss (Cf. *Brahmasūtrabhāṣya*, I, 1, 11; I, 1, 20); and that Advaitins, in their analysis of the self, clearly describe a level of harmony in experience that is associated ontologically with *saguṇa* Brahman (see Chapter IV).

experience itself. Brahman is not *saccidānanda*, if by designating Brahman as *saccidānanda* one does intend to ascribe a positive character to Brahman. As "oneness," no wholly true affirmations (or negations) can be made about Brahman. Human language is grounded in a phenomenal experience of multiplicity and cannot therefore be used accurately to refer to Brahman; likewise, human logic is based upon phenomenal experience and thus is incapable of "determining," without at the same time "negating," its subject. This condition which the mind finds itself subject to leads to the necessity to distinguish two forms, as it were, of Brahman: Brahman as it is in itself, *nirguṇa* Brahman, or Brahman without quality; and Brahman as it is conceived by man from his limited phenomenal standpoint, *saguṇa* Brahman, or Brahman with qualities. The affirmation of *saguṇa* Brahman, however, is not merely an acknowledgment of human limitations; it is also the name for that spiritual experience that harmonizes rather than obliterates distinctions. *Saguṇa* Brahman is the "content" of a loving experience of unity; *nirguṇa* Brahman is the "content" of an intuitive experience of identity. *Saguṇa* Brahman is not the highest possible form of experience; nevertheless, it is an extremely valuable experience in that it enables the Advaitin to affirm on one level of being the essential spirituality of everything that has being.

2 Levels of Being

Reality is that which cannot be *subrated* by any other experience.

Appearance is that which can be *subrated* by other experience.

Unreality is that which neither can nor cannot be *subrated* by other experience.

I

What is the mental process through which men generate their ontologies, their ordering of experience in terms of the concept of "being"? And how can this process be employed as a criterion for the making of distinctions between "orders of being"? The Advaitic answer to this is embodied in the Sanskrit term *bādha*—which means "contradiction" and, in the context of Advaita ontology, is often translated as "cancellation" or "sublation." For purposes of clarity and for drawing out its meaning more fully, this concept may be reconstructed as *subration*.

Subration is the mental process whereby one disvalues some previously appraised object or content of consciousness because of its being contradicted by a new experience. A judgment about something is contradicted by a new experience when it is impossible—more as a psychological fact of one's being than as a purely logical state of one's mind—to affirm (to act upon or to orient one's attitudes upon) both the previous judgment and what is learned or acquired in the new experience. From the standpoint of the subject, *to subrate* means to undergo an experience—practical, intellectual, or spiritual—which radically changes one's judgment about something. An object or content of consciousness is *subrated* or is *subrat-*

able when it is or can be so disvaluated, denied, or contradicted by another experience.

When one sees a figure in a wax museum and takes it for a living person, and then later discovers (perhaps because of its inability to respond to one's attention) that it is not a living person but a wax figure, one has subrated one's prior experience of the object: one has rejected one's initial judgment of it and replaced that judgment with another which, one believes, conforms with reality.

Subration is thus a mental process through which one rectifies errors; but not all rectifications of error come under this process. Suppose one believes that a certain idea, say, a mathematical concept, will work in a certain situation, that it will be applicable to the solving of some particular problem, but then discovers that it doesn't work. Here, an error of judgment has been made and has been recognized; but subration has not occured. Subration requires a turning away from, or rejection of, an object or content of consciousness as initially appraised in the light of a new judgment or experience which takes the place of the earlier judgment and to which "belief" is attached. It is an *axio-noetic* process that involves, psychologically, a withdrawal of attention from an object as it was originally judged to be and the fastening of attention either to the same object as reappraised or to another object that replaces the first object as a content of consciousness; and the placing of a higher value upon the content of the new judgment.

Subration involves: (1) a judgment about some object or content of consciousness (a material thing, a person, an idea); (2) the recognition, in the light of another kind of judgment that is incompatible with the initial judgment, that the initial judgment is faulty; and (3) the acceptance of the new judgment as valid. Subration is a distinctive mental process whose distinguishing feature is a revision of judgment about something so that the former judgment is radically denied by a new judgment that is based on fresh insight or experience. The judging process itself is not simply an axiological one of the sort "X, which I thought to be good, is bad," or "X, which I believed to be important, is unimportant"; it is, rather, an axio-noetic one of the sort "X, because of *a*, *b*, *c*, . . . is to be rejected and replaced by Y," where X and Y may be concepts, existential relations, physical objects, etc. From the viewpoint of the subject, subration is destructive of the object as previously judged: the object is no longer capable of eliciting one's interest or commanding one's attention.[1]

Containing, then, as it does, both axiological and noetic dimensions that are brought together into a functional synthesis, subration is uniquely qualified, according to Advaita, to serve as a criterion for the making of ontological distinctions. When something is subrated, one believes it to have a lesser degree or kind of "reality" than that which takes its place. In terms of subration, one's experience dictates that the more something is capable of being subrated, the less reality it has, or the more reality something has, the less capable it is of being subrated.

1 A simple valuation or judgment of the sort "X is good" involves, to be sure, certain epistemic features. It presupposes some knowledge of what is evaluated and some kind of cognitive comparison between the evaluated object and other possibilities. It does not involve, however, an explicit rejection of an object as initially evaluated and the replacement of it by something else. Subration does involve these special noetic qualities; specific reasons are carried along as part and parcel of the rejecting-replacing process. They are brought forth by the very experience of insight which, because of its richer content, condemns the initial object-as-judged to the realm of the rejected.

Further, there can be no such thing as *gradual* subration. There might indeed be a considerable process of doubting and evaluating leading up to it, but the actual act of subration is integral and, by its nature, radical. Subration occurs only when a contradiction between two kinds of judgment or experience is recognized, which recognition, psychologically speaking, is immediate.

II

Reality is that which cannot be subrated by any other experience.

We are, by the conditions of our mental being, compelled to ascribe "Reality" to that which, in fact and in principle, cannot be disvaluated, denied, or contradicted by anything else. For if Reality were applicable to everything, that is to say, if the term were applied to any object without this qualification, then it would cease to perform any useful philosophical function.[2] The Advaitin, however, is immediately placed in this difficulty, which he can readily acknowledge, that he is not so much able to justify his calling something "real" on the basis of subration as he is to explicate a conception of reality by the use of subration as an ontological criterion. Logically, or, better, linguistically, the Advaitin would still maintain that if the term "reality" is to have any distinctive philosophical significance or special ontological meaning, it must refer to that "content" which is non-subratable, to that content which is disclosed in the highest form or quality of our human experience. And the experience which discloses that content ceases to be "human" in any narrow sense of the word.

The only experience, or state of being, whose content cannot be subrated in fact and in principle by any other experience—which no other experience can conceivably contradict—is the experience of pure spiritual identity; the experience wherein the separation of self and non-self, of ego and world, is transcended, and pure oneness alone remains. This is the experience celebrated by the Advaitin as one of perfect insight, bliss, and power; as one of infinite joy and understanding. In spiritual identity (*nirvikalpa*

2 One could, indeed, as a matter of terminological convenience, use the term "reality" to apply to everything, provided that one introduced "degrees" of reality as they are determined by subration. This usage, however, according to Advaita, would tend to confound, rather than to clarify, certain differences in kind that emerge from the application of the criterion of subration.

samādhi) the pretensions to ultimacy of anything else are shattered, and a complete self-realization and self-knowledge are said to be obtained. What kind of experience could conceivably subrate unqualified identity—the experience of absolute value wherein the unique oneness of being stands forth as the sole content of consciousness? Sureśvara, a ninth-century Advaitin, puts it thus:

> Wheresoever there, is doubt, there, the wise should know, the Self [the Real] is not. For no doubts can arise in relation to the Self, since its nature is pure immediate consciousness.[3]

Subration requires the presence of an object or content of consciousness that can be contradicted by other experience: Reality as non-dual, in terms of a phenomenology of experience as well as by definition, denies the possibility of there being some other "object" that could replace it. Just as Spinoza's "substance" cannot be conceived in terms other than itself, being the whole that includes but transcends all parts, so the Advaitin's Reality cannot be denied by anything drawn from lower orders of experience: by its nature as oneness, no distinctions can be applied to it, and all ordinary valuations, which presuppose a distinction between subject and object, must be suspended when confronting it.[4]

By the criterion of subration, then, *Reality* is that which *is* when the subject/object situation is transcended. *The Real* is that which is the content of non-dual spiritual experience. It is the timeless, unconditioned, undifferentiated oneness of being. The Real is (*nirguṇa*) Brahman.

3 *Naiṣkarmya Siddhi*, III, 37, trans. by A. J. Alston (London: Shanti Sadan, 1959).

4 Cf. Śaṁkara, *Brahmasūtrabhāṣya*, II, 1, 14. "... As long as something else remains a desire is possible; but there is nothing else which could be desired in addition to the absolute unity of Brahman.... [Consciousness of unity] is seen to have for its result the cessation of ignorance, ... there is no other kind of knowledge by which it could be sublated." —*The Vedānta-Sūtras with the Commentary of Śaṅkarācārya*, trans. by George Thibaut, *op.cit.*

III

Appearance is that which can be subrated by other experience.

Three types of "existents" need to be distinguished within the domain of Appearance: types which, categorically speaking, exhaust the domain. These are:

1. The "real existent," which comprises those contents of experience that can be subrated only by Reality. For example:

a) Among "existential relations"—those relational experiences such as theistic religious experience and experience of love in which the experiencer believes and reports that his experience is a genuine relational experience between self and God or another person and that it is a fulfilling one.

A relational experience that is founded on the distinction between self and non-self—where the non-self is taken to be God or another person to whom one offers oneself in loving relation and in which the experience fulfills the emotional-intellectual-spiritual demands made upon it—cannot be subrated by another experience within the subject/object situation because, by its nature it has already been valued as among the highest in the order of sense-mental experience; that is to say, it has been valued commensurate with the fulfillment that it yields. But this relational experience can be subrated by Reality, by an experience that transcends the dualistic distinctions upon which that relation is founded; for when pure identity shines forth as the content of consciousness, all distinctions and all experience constituted by these distinctions are necessarily cancelled.

b) Among "particular objects"—those objects that, by the manner in which they were brought into being and are responded to, "participate" in Reality and at the same time retain a distinctive nature of their own; e.g., a work of art. Without elaborating a theory of aesthetics, one can confidently say that inherent in the nature of (and definition of) a successful aesthetic experience is the valuation of it as belonging to the highest order of sense-mental experience. One who experiences a work of art and who feels that his experience is successful, that it provides integration and insight, values that experience in ways which rule out its being contradicted and replaced by another kind of sense-mental experience.[5] A work of art, then, which is so capable of eliciting this kind of response, is subratable only through the realization that no work of art is comparable to the splendor of Reality; that no work of art can fully grasp that splendor or transmit it to others.

c) Among "concepts"—those logical relations, such as the law of contradiction, that have a necessary, indispensable function in organizing and making possible propositional truth. These concepts, by definition, cannot be denied or contradicted by other sense-mental experience. What is logically necessary cannot be denied by a mind that is committed in advance to its use.

The real existent represents the highest kind of experience or object within Appearance. The real existent is subratable only by experience of Reality wherein any ultimacy that was previously attached to it is denied: it is subratable only by what is qualitatively different in kind from it.

2. The second order of being within Appearance may be called the "existent." It comprises those contents of experience that can be subrated by Reality or by the real existent. For example:

a) Among "existential relations"—those relational experiences such as casual encounters with other persons in which the

5 Experientially, there is no alternative to an experience that fulfills the intellectual-emotional demands made upon it in the sense that no other experience of a like or lesser nature can replace it. A work of art that is experienced satisfactorily is not replaced by another work of art or by another kind of sense-mental experience. One might indeed turn from a work of art, upon the "completion" of one's experience of it, to another work of art or to something else. The second work or object, however, does not axio-noetically deny the first, for there need be no incompatibility between them.

merely conventional or the purely formal predominates. These experiences can be subrated by the more fulfilling experiences that involve relations between persons as inviolable, subjective centers, as *persons* with intrinsic, and not simply instrumental, worth. Experience testifies that once one attains this deeper, more embracing and vital level of relationship, the merely conventional or formal aspect of relationship at that time is contradicted and is replaced by that deeper experience.

b) Among "particular objects"—any particular *qua* particular; any object, that is, which is taken as an *independent* reality. These objects are subrated by the real existent the moment one realizes and affirms the interdependence and interpenetration of all particulars. The particular *qua* particular is subrated, in short, when the relations that the particular has to things and to processes that are external to it become the content of experience. Once one realizes that any particular has its being in, and through, its relations with other particulars and processes, with Nature or existence as a whole, that it is a *dependent* being, the otherwise absolute separativeness and uniqueness of the particular is contradicted and is replaced by that more universal realization.

c) Among "concepts"—those logical relations such as might be employed in a purely formal logistic system. Logical relations that lack necessity and that function entirely as analytic statements are subratable by those relations that do, in mental experience, have necessity (e.g., the law of contradiction). By definition, formal or "conventional" relations function successfully only within restricted systems (of logic, mathematics, geometry . . .).[6]

6 Because of their functioning within restricted systems, one would not speak of these "existent" concepts as being subratable by other like concepts—for again there is no incompatibility between relations within different systems. One can accept these various relations each in its place. In other words, logical (or mathematical, geometrical) relations that have a purely formal character are not rejected relative to the

These kinds of existential relations, objects, and concepts can be subrated by Reality, wherein they would simply disappear as contents worthy of final consideration; or by the real existent, wherein they would be supplanted by it. The vast majority of sense-mental experience comes within the existent type of Appearance. The everyday contacts with physical things, the presuppositions, habits, conventional beliefs and opinions that govern most mental activity, the indifferent relations with other persons—all are data of experience, contents of consciousness, which have objective significance but which can be disvaluated, denied, and contradicted by any experience and insight which brings one closer to what is ontologically true or logically necessary.

3. The third order within Appearance is the "illusory existent." It comprises those contents of experience that can be subrated by all other types of experience. Hallucinations, pure fancies and dreams, erroneous sense-perceptions, and the like are "illusory": they may be vivid experiences, but they fail to satisfy certain basic practical or intellectual needs: they lack empirical truth.

A relationship is an illusory existent when one is simply mistaken about what one is relating with (mainly to the extent that it is incapable of responding to one in the manner assumed), as when one mistakes a shadow and noise for a burglar. A physical object is an illusory existent when it is simply mis-perceived, as when one mistakingly believes that a log is an alligator. A concept is an illusory existent when it fails to satisfy the functions intended by it, as when through ignorance of the rules of a language one formulates an analytically false statement which was intended to function as a genuine analytic statement. These relations, objects, and con-

special system in which they function when one chooses a different system to apply to a specific case; e.g., the choosing of a non-Euclidian geometry in a given physical theory. It is only when necessity is attached to relations irrespective of their functioning in a special system, and this no doubt occurs but rarely, that subration of this type occurs.

cepts can be subrated by existent experience, wherein their illusory quality would stand revealed; or, again, by the real existent and Reality.

All contents of sense-mental experience, of experience wherein a fundamental distinction exists between subject and object, are susceptible to this stripping away of values previously imposed upon them because of their incompatibility with other forms of experience, and to this turning away from them as objects no longer worthy of one's consideration. As human experience testifies, any judgment within Appearance, any experience, or belief or idea that is subject to a mental perspective—to external conditions—which is bound up with temporal determinations can, in principle, be falsified by future experience. Any experience of the self who has not attained Reality is subject to being rejected by a qualitatively higher experience.[7]

Appearance, then, comprises that about which doubts can arise. It is that which is, or in principle can be, a datum of experience within the subject/object situation. *The Apparent* is that which is the content of sense-mental experience. It is the differentiated multiplicity of being.

IV

Unreality is that which neither can nor cannot be subrated by other experience.

An "object" is unreal when, because of its self-contradictoriness, it cannot appear as a datum of experience. A square circle, the daughter of a virgin, and the like are objects that have a conceptual status only, namely, as contradictions: that which is denoted by such terms (and here one assumes that the terms were not intended to function as analytic statements, in the first place,

7 Every datum of experience within Appearance is "existent," however, and not "unreal," according to the Advaitin, so far as it is a datum of experience; that is, as it is a concrete fact of our experience. It nevertheless lacks full reality because it is subratable.

in which case they would come under the classification of the illusory existent) is necessarily non-existent; it is incapable of coming into concrete being as an object with which one can interact.

The illusory existent is that which, in fact, does not have an objective counterpart; the Unreal is that which, in principal, cannot have an objective counterpart.[8] Our human experience shows that all actual sense-mental experience of self and non-self is subject mentally to the law of contradiction. By definition certain objects are denied the possibility of possessing existence, of being objects of actual human experience.

Unreality is that which can never be a content of experience. By the criterion of subration, the *Unreal* is non-being.

V

The three fundamental modes of being, Reality, Appearance, and Unreality, are—from the standpoint of reason and experience—incommensurable; qualitatively they are different in kind. Reality, Appearance, and Unreality thus constitute *levels of being* between which reason is impotent to establish causal relations.[9]

This hierarchical ontology, though, holds only from the standpoint of Appearance: from the standpoint of Reality, no other

8 Further, the "illusory existent" always points to an empirically real existent, whereas the Unreal cannot point to anything. The "alligator" indicates the existence of the log and is dependent upon it; the "square circle" neither points to, nor is experientially dependent upon, a circle or circular object.

9 The term "level" seems to function in discourse primarily as a spatial metaphor: in common language it connotes "aboves" and "belows"—one forms an image of "levels" by thinking of one thing as being above or below another thing or of one thing as being "deeper" than another thing, as in the expression "levels of meaning." The term "level," however, for purposes of ontology, can be given a more precise conceptual meaning. Two orders of being can be said to be on different levels: (1) when, epistemologically, because of differences in kind between them (temporal, qualitative, etc.), relations cannot be established rationally between them; (2) when, logically, assertions made about one of the orders from the standpoint of the other may legitimately violate

kinds of being are present that can be distinguished. In other words, from the standpoint of Reality there is no distinction between Appearance and Unreality, or between Itself and anything else: from the standpoint of Reality there is and can be only Reality.

The distinctions between Reality and Appearance, and between Appearance and Unreality, and between Reality and Unreality, according to Advaita, may be necessary and valid as mental organizations of experience from the standpoint of rational-sense consciousness. The distinctions, in short, may be justified as "philosophy"; albeit they are rejected in Reality. The distinctions are themselves subratable and hence are confined to the order of Appearance.[10]

the formal requirements that govern the thought of the one order when confined to itself (e.g., assertions about the Godhead or Absolute in religious literature made from the empirical standpoint may legitimately violate—and they frequently do—the law of contradiction); and (3) when, axiologically, different grades of value are ascribed to the orders. A level of being thus has special and distinguishing espistemological, logical, and axiological characteristics. Ontologically, levels exist when reason cannot establish relations (causal and other) between two orders of being; when formal principles of logic can be suspended when asserting something across these orders; and when different values are given to them. Reality is "higher" than Appearance, not because Reality is located spatially above Appearance, but because Reality is incommensurable with Appearance, because thought when directed to it is able to make meaningful statements that do violate the necessary principles of thought that are grounded in Appearance, and because a greater value is ascribed to it.

10 We have tried in this chapter to articulate in very concise terms the ontological levels affirmed by Advaita Vedānta and to show how these are arrived at and how they are constituted. Śaṁkara, in his various works, explicitly acknowledges three levels: *paramārthika* (which corresponds precisely to the level of Reality), *vyavahārika* (which includes all the sublevels of Appearance except the "illusory existent"), and *pratibhāṣika* (which is the "illusory existent"). The term "*vyavahārika*" will be introduced in the next chapter in what we take to be its correct technical philosophical context. The level of "Unreality" is implicitly accepted by Śaṁkara, although it is not usually treated in the "levels of being" as such. The sublevel of the "real existent" is not clearly formulated in Advaitic literature, but it is implied, we believe, by the divisions that are established and is explicitly affirmed in other contexts especially in its epistemic dimension.

3 Brahman and the World

As a spider spreads and withdraws (its thread) . . . so out of the Immutable does the phenomenal universe arise.[1]

Crave to know that from which all beings take birth, that from which being born they live, and that towards which they move and into which they merge. That is Brahman.[2]

One of the most basic questions taken up in the Upaniṣads, which later becomes perhaps the central problem of classical, systematic Vedānta, is: What is the relation that obtains between Brahman and the world? Or in what sense is Brahman, the Absolute, the creator of the world? The Upaniṣadic answer to this question is multiform.[3] Numerous descriptions of creation are proffered, most of which follow a Sāṁkhyan-type model of emanation.[4] At the same time the Upaniṣads affirm repeatedly that Brahman is "one only without a second," that Brahman is a state of being wherein all distinctions between self, world, and God are transcended and are obliterated.[5] Classical Advaita Vedānta likewise treats the question in various ways and suggests different answers to it. There

1 *Muṇḍaka Upaniṣad* I, 1, 7.

2 *Taittirīya Upaniṣad,* III, 1, 1.

3 E.g., *Chāndogya Upaniṣad,* III, 19, 1, and VI, 2, 1–4ff. *Aitareya Upaniṣad,* I, 1. *Praśna Upaniṣad,* I, 4. *Bṛhad-āraṇyaka Upaniṣad,* I, 2, 1, and I, 4, 1.

4 The Sāṁkhya model of emanation consists in a progressive unfolding of various principles, such as mind (*manas*) and egoity (*ahaṁkāra*), out of a primordial nature (*prakṛti*), which then form the basis of the subtle and gross objects that constitute the world. For a good introduction to this system, cf. A. Berriedale Keith, *The Sāṁkhya System* ("The Heritage of India Series" [Calcutta: YMCA Publishing House, 1949]).

5 E.g., *Kaṭha Upaniṣad,* II, 1, 1. *Chāndogya Upaniṣad,* VI, 2, 1. *Kena Upaniṣad,* I, 4.

is nevertheless a substantial core of doctrine and attitude that is shared by most, if not all, Advaitins. Following Śaṁkara, these Advaitins explain the relation between Brahman and the world in terms of *satkāryavāda*, the theory that the effect pre-exists in its cause, with Brahman (as Īśvara "the Lord") as the material and efficient cause of the world; and in terms of *vivartavāda*, the theory that the effect is only an apparent manifestation of its cause. These theories have their background in the concepts of *māyā* (illusion), *avidyā* (ignorance), and *adhyāsa* (superimposition).

I

In the immediate, intuitive experience of non-duality, Brahman presents itself as the fullness of being, as self-luminous consciousness, and as infinite bliss (*saccidānanda*). The complex world of our ordinary experience disappears in the pure white light of a spiritual simplicity. All distinctions, contradictions, and multiplicities are transcended and are obliterated. In Brahman-experience (*nirvikalpa samādhi*), as has been pointed out, there is the awareness that true reality belongs only to the content of that experience; that "anything beside Brahman lacks full reality."

It follows, then, that the existence of, or our perception of, an independent, substantial world of real objects, persons, and processes must be grounded in some pervasive error. We take the unreal for the real and the real for the unreal. This is *māyā*.

Whenever the "I," "me," or "mine" is present, according to Advaita, there also is *māyā*. *Māyā* is all experience that is constituted by, and follows from, the distinction between subject and object, between self and non-self.

Whenever we transform the impersonal into the personal, that is, when we make Brahman something or someone who cares, we bring about an association of the impersonal with *māyā*. *Māyā* is the ontic-noetic state wherein limitations (*upādhis*) are imposed upon Reality.

All attachments, aversions, fears, dreams, and semidreams are touched with *māyā*. All memories, cognitions, percepts, and logics are grounded in *māyā*. *Māyā* is whenever we fail to realize the oneness of the Real.

And *māyā* is beginningless (*anādi*), for time arises only within it; it is unthinkable (*acintya*), for all thought is subject to it; it is indescribable (*anirvacanīya*), for all language results from it. The level of Appearance is thus *māyā*.

Advaita Vedānta explicates the notion of *māyā* from two perspectives, the metaphysical and the epistemological. Before we proceed with the explication, however, it is necessary that we call attention to the peculiar manner in which Advaitins often treat problems at once in metaphysical and epistemological terms and use these perspectives as correctives to each other. Not infrequently (and, according to its detractors, whenever the going gets rough), the Advaitin will raise a problem such as "creation" in essentially metaphysical terms and then, after proposing an answer to it which harmonizes with "scripture" (*śruti*), go on to treat it in epistemological terms—in terms essentially of a phenomenology of noetic-consciousness and of multi-level epistemic standpoints. This turning to the epistemological as a "corrective" to the metaphysical is not, however, as far as the Advaitin is concerned, to turn "positivistic"; rather the turning is intended to bring one to a fuller awareness and understanding of reality itself. In other words, the epistemological analysis does not seek to destroy the metaphysical claim, but to support and complement it. And the primary claim that all Advaitic thought seeks to support is that of the sole reality of Brahman. This objective leads the Advaitin to analyze experience in terms of the various levels of being. From the standpoint of Brahman-experience itself, there is no question about, or problem of, creation, for in this experience or state of being there is no distinction between creator and created: creation is a question and problem only from the standpoint of rational-empirical consciousness, from the standpoint of Appearance within which philosophizing takes place. The shifting from one level to another in the treatment of a problem is characteristic of Advaitic Vedānta, and it fulfills the purpose of leading the mind from one level of experience (the Apparent) to another (the Real). In short, the primary intent of the Advaitic analysis of the relation that obtains between Brahman and the world is to lead the mind beyond the level of asking the question to the level of seeing the answer.

Following the ancient Vedic usage of *māyā* as a mysterious, deceptive power of the gods,[6] the Advaitin, metaphysically conceives of *māyā* as that power (*śakti*) of Brahman by which the world of multiplicity comes into existence. *Māyā* is a creative power until one realizes the truth of the sole reality of Brahman. One of the analogies favored by the Advaitin to clarify this is that of the magician and his trick; and here already a transition is made into the epistemological. When a magician makes one thing appear as something else, or when he seemingly produces something from nothing, we are deluded by it; we mistake appearance for reality—but not the magician. For us the illusion is caused by the power of the magician and by our ignorance; for the magician there is no illusion at all. And just as the magician creates illusions that are not binding upon him and that last as long as the experiencer is in ignorance, so Brahman conjures up a world show of phenomena that disappears upon the attainment of knowledge (*jñāna*, *vidyā*). Metaphysically, *māyā* is that mysterious power of Brahman that deludes us into taking the empirical world as reality. Epistemologically, *māyā* is ignorance (*avidyā*). It has the power of concealing reality (*āvaraṇa-śakti*) and also of misrepresenting or distorting

6 E.g., *Ṛg Veda*, III, 53, 8, and VI, 47, 18.

reality (*vikṣepa-śakti*).[7] Not only do we fail to perceive Brahman, but we also substitute something else in its place, viz., the phenomenal world. *Māyā* is thus not merely a negative designation, a privation of vision; it is positive so far as it produces an illusion (*bhāva rūpam ajñānam*).

For Advaita Vedānta, then, the phenomenal world is *māyā*, and it is produced by *māyā*. But it is not on that account merely a figment of one's imagination. With the possible exception of Prakāśānanda, Advaitic thinkers hold that a subjective idealism is not the proper philosophical expression or consequence of a doctrine of *māyā*. So far as a separate subject exists, so does the object that is experienced by it. Duality is transcended only in an experience that is different in kind from what takes place in the subject/object situation. Śaṁkara writes:

> There could be no non-existence (of external entities) because external entities are actually perceived. . . .
>
> An external entity is invariably perceived in every cognition such as pillar, wall, a pot or a piece of cloth. It can never be that what is actually perceived is non-existent.[8]

7 This distinction of the two powers of *māyā* is usually attributed to Maṇḍana Miśra, the founder of the Bhāmatī school of Advaita.

8 Śaṁkara, *Brahmasūtrabhāṣya,* II, 2, 28, in *Brahma-Sūtra-Shānkara-Bhāshya,* trans. by V. M. Apte (Bombay: Popular Book Depot, 1960). Śaṁkara's attack on subjective idealism is, in this context, directed against the *vijñānavāda* school of Buddhism, which did uphold the position that the contents of empirical consciousness could be accounted for entirely in terms of the activities of consciousness alone. The realism of Advaita is in opposition to this position both on theoretical and practical grounds. It is argued theoretically that subject/object experience means precisely a distinction between subject and object, which distinction can be overcome only through transcendence; and practically that any doctrine of subjectivism becomes a barrier to this act of transcendence.

In later Vedānta, however, a kind of subjectivism called *dṛṣṭisṛṣṭi-vāda* ("doctrine that perception is creation") was put forward (by Prakāśānanda), but it was argued for in a somewhat different philosophical context, and, in any event, it would clearly have been rejected by Śaṁkara and his early followers. (Cf. Appaya Dīkṣita, *Siddhāntaleśa-saṁgraha,* 3:711.)

No one, in other words, perceives merely his own perception: existence must be attributed to external objects because they are cognized as such. The world, then, "appears to be real as long as the non-dual Brahman, which is the basis of all, is not known."[9]

What is meant then by calling the world an illusion and at the same time ascribing existence to it? The answer is that for Advaita Vedānta the term "real" means that which is permanent, eternal, infinite, that which is *trikālābādhyam*, never subrated at any time by another experience—and Brahman alone fits this meaning. The world then is not real, but it is not wholly unreal. The unreal or non-being, as we have seen, is that which never appears as an objective datum of experience because of its self-contradictoriness. In the words of the *Bhagavadgītā*: "... of the non-real there is no coming to be; of the real there is no ceasing to be."[10] The world that is distinguished from true reality (*sat*) and from complete non-reality (*asat*) has then an apparent or practical reality, which is called *vyavahārika*. *Vyavahārika* is the level of *māyā* that denotes the totality or errors caused by *avidyā*. It is *sadasadvilakṣaṇa*, other than the real or the unreal; or *anirvacanīya*, indescribable in terms of being and non-being.[11]

9 *Ibid.*

10 *Bhagavadgītā*, II, 16.

11 It is necessary to emphasize this rather strongly because Advaita Vedānta has so often been presented to the West as a philosophy that simply condemns the world to unreality. For Advaita, the world, from the standpoint of reason or subject/object consciousness, is neither real nor unreal (as these terms have been defined): the world is an illusion only on the basis of an experience of the Absolute. The world cannot be an illusion to one who lacks that experience. Empirical reality, in other words, is transcended only absolutely. Only from the viewpoint of the infinite does everything but itself appear as without substance, without independent reality and value. In short: "there is no reason to call the world unreal *before* the knowledge of the oneness of the Ātman (has been attained)." (Sureśvara, *Saṁbandha Vārttika*, as quoted by N. K. Devaraja in *An Introduction to Śaṁkara's Theory of Knowledge* (Delhi: Motilal Banarsidas, 1962), p. 16.

Both in the writings of Śaṁkara and in those of post-Śaṁkara Advaitins, the terms "*māyā*" and "*avidyā*" come to be used interchangeably, with *avidyā* actually taking precedence over *māyā* in the explanation of bondage and freedom. When asked, "What is the cause of our bondage, of our not realizing Brahman?" the answer most frequently given is *avidyā*, ignorance.[12] And in describing the process of *avidyā*, Śaṁkara introduces one of his most significant and interesting notions, that of *adhyāsa* (also later termed *adhyāropa*), which means "superimposition."

In the Introduction to his commentary on the *Brahma-sūtras*, Śaṁkara defines superimposition as the "apparent presentation (*avabhāsa*) [to consciousness] by way of rememberance (*smṛtirūpaḥ*) of something previously perceived (*pūrvadṛṣṭa*) in something else (*paratra*)." "It is," he goes on to say, "the unreal assumption about the attributes of one thing as being the attributes of some other thing." And again, *adhyāsa* "is the notion of *that* in something which is *not-that*: just as it is, for example, when a person superimposes on his self attributes external to his own self. . . ." Superimposition takes place, then, when the qualities of one thing not immediately present to consciousness are, through memory, given to, or projected upon, another thing that is present to consciousness and are identified with it. In the stock example of the rope and the snake, the rope (the thing immediately present to consciousness) is taken as a snake through the erroneous attribution of qualities

12 Two forms of *avidyā* are frequently distinguished in Advaita Vedānta: a *mūla* or primeval, universal, and a *tula* or temporary *avidyā*. The distinction enables the Advaitin to account for a common empirical world (in terms of *mūlāvidyā*) and an individual world of temporary illusions (in terms of *tulāvidyā*).

In later Advaita the question also is raised about the locus (*āśraya*) of *avidyā*. Is it the *jīva*, the individual self, or Brahman, the universal self? The Bhāmatī school argues for the *jīva*, and the Vivaraṇa school, for Brahman. Both schools hold, though, that *avidyā* lasts just so long as the truth of Brahman has not been realized and that once this truth is realized, all spatio-temporal questions about *avidyā* are meaningless.

remembered from previous perceptions (of snakes). The judgment that expresses this illusion, i.e., the judgment, "this is a snake," is the result of a positive identification between what is remembered and what is perceived.[13]

The main or primary application of *adhyāsa* is made with respect to the self. It is the superimposition on the Self (Ātman, Brahman) of what does not properly belong to the Self (finitude, change) and the superimposition on the non-self of what does properly belong to the Self (infinitude, eternality) that constitute *avidyā*. "It is by adopting the reciprocal superimposition of the self and the non-self," writes Śaṁkara, "that all world conduct and Vedic (ritualistic) actions ... are promoted." Vidyāraṇa in his *Pañcadaśī* asks: "What is the obstruction that prevents the recognition of the self?" And answers: "It is the superimposition of what does not really exist and is not self-evident on the Self. . . ."[14] And: "Those who do not see clearly attribute causation to Brahman, and assign the characteristics of Brahman, such as existence, to Ishvara, the creator of the universe."[15]

II

Brahman, or Īśvara (Brahman with attributes; Brahman become personalized as Deity), is said to be the cause of the world, then, so far as Brahman is the ground or locus of all superimpositions; so far, that is to say, as we are subject to *māyā*, *avidyā*. A

13 Padmapāda, in his early commentary on Śaṁkara's work, explains simply that "superimposition means the manifestation of the nature of something in another which is not of that nature." "As in [the statement] 'I am deaf.' Deafness is the property of the organ of hearing and not of the self."—*Pañcapādikā*, V, 12 and VII, 17, trans. by D. Venkataramiah ("Gaekwad's Oriental Series," Vol. CVII [Bangalore: 1948]).

14 *Panchadasi* [*Pañcadaśī*], I, 13, trans. by Hari Prasad Shastri (London: Shanti Sadan, 1956).

15 *Ibid.*, VI, 192.

special application of *adhyāsa* is just this superimposition of activity upon Brahman and the superimposition of effects upon causes. We assume that the cause (Brahman) actually transforms itself into an effect (the world of change and multiplicity) or that the effect, having an independent reality, is radically different in nature from the cause.

This brings us back to the central question, What is the relation that obtains between Brahman and the world? The Advaitic answer to this question, with its background in *māyā*, *avidyā*, and *adhyāsa*, is set forth in terms of two closely interrelated theories: the general theory of *satkāryavāda*, the theory that the effect pre-exists in its cause; and the special theory of *vivartavāda*, that the effect is only a manifestation or appearance of the cause.[16]

Before these theories are taken up in our own terms, in order to understand their philosophical import it is necessary that some of the specific arguments that have been put forward in their behalf be examined first. Śaṁkara argues first of all that *satkāryavāda*—the theory that an effect is nothing more than its material cause (*upādāna kāraṇa*) and ontologically is not-different (*ananya*) from it—corresponds to the actual facts of perceptual experience; that perception presents the relation between (material) cause and effect as one of non-difference.

16 The opposite of *satkāryavāda* in Indian philosophy is *asatkāryavāda*, which is generally held by Buddhism, Mīmāṁsā, and Nyāya-Vaiśeṣika; the opposite or opposing view to *vivartavāda* (within the framework of *satkāryavāda*) is *pariṇāmavāda*, the theory of transformation held by the Sāṁkhya system. We have then:

satkāryavāda	*asatkāryavāda*
Effect pre-exists in cause (Advaita and Sāṁkhya)	Effect exists independent of cause (Buddhism, Mīmāṁsā, Nyāya-Vaiśeṣika)

vivarta-vāda	*pariṇāma-vāda*
(Advaita)	(Sāṁkhya)
Effect is mere "appearance"	Effect is actual "transformation"

> Such non-difference between cause and effect does happen to be directly perceived. It is this way: – In the case of a cloth which is a construction of threads, we do not of course perceive merely an effect, viz., the cloth as such, as apart from the threads themselves, but what we actually and directly see are merely the threads only in their condition as warps and woofs . . . .[17]

This fact of our perception is further supported, according to Śaṁkara, by practical experience. If particular effects were not already latent in particular causes, then it would be possible for any given effect to issue from any cause; and this is clearly not the case.

> Our ordinary experience tells us that milk, clay and gold are taken by people in order to produce out of them curds, jars, and ornaments, respectively. No one who wants curds will expect to have it out of clay, nor will anyone expect to have jars out of milk. This means that the effect exists in the cause prior to its production. For had the effect been really non-existent before its production, there is no reason why curds [could not] be produced out of milk alone or jars out of clay. Besides, all the effects being equally non-existent, anything might come out of anything else.[18]

In further criticism of *asatkāryavāda* (the theory that effects do not pre-exist in their causes), Śaṁkara argues that it would lead to an infinite regress (*anavasthā*), for the granting of independence to two distinct realities—the cause and the effect—requires the positing of a third entity which is the relation of invariable concommitance that holds between them. And then this third entity (which must be distinct from the two terms that it relates) requires a fourth relating entity that would relate the third entity with each of the first two terms, and so on to a fifth, sixth, ...

17 *Brahmasūtrabhāṣya,* II, 1, 15, trans. by V. M. Apte, *op.cit.*

18 *Ibid.,* II, 1, 18, in *Vedānta Explained, Śaṅkara's Commentary on The Brahmasūtras,* trans. by V. H. Date (Bombay: Bookseller's Publishing Co., 1954).

> Even in the assumption of a Samavāya relation (invariable concommitance) if it is understood that there is a relation as between the Samavāya, on the one hand, and the two entities between which such Samavāya exists ..., on the other, then such another Samavāya relation of that, and then still such another Samavāya relation of that, *ad infinitum,* will have to be imagined, and hence the predicament of a *regressus ad infinitum* would result . . . .[19]

The last major argument that Śaṁkara uses is also drawn from experience. He argues that a mere change in outward form does not constitute a fundamental change in substance. An effect, to be sure, is different from its cause in outward appearance, for otherwise no distinction would be made in the first place. But this does not mean that there are two distinct realities, the one "cause," the other "effect." A change in form is not a change in reality, for in spite of changes in form, a substance is recognized as a single reality.

> A thing as such does not become another different thing altogether, by merely appearing in a different aspect. Devadatta, whose hands and legs are (at one time) in a fixed position, and Devadatta whose hands and legs are (at some other time) in an extended position, and who is thus seen to be in such different attitudes (at different times), does not merely on that account become different persons, because he is still recognizable as the same one person.[20]

III

But what do these arguments actually prove? They establish that within the phenomenal world one cannot make an ontological distinction between cause and effect; that an effect is nothing but a set of conditions, that it is nothing but the cause itself, albeit seen

19 *Ibid.,* trans. by V. M. Apte, *op.cit.*
20 *Ibid.*

in a different form or state: the arguments do not prove anything as far as the relation between the world and Brahman is concerned; they suggest only that the world may be seen as an effect of Brahman, which is Brahman itself in a different form.

The main purport of the arguments establishing *satkāryavāda* therefore is practical. In terms of the requirements of spiritual experience, it is believed that without the extension of Brahman in the world (Brahman in this context becoming Īśvara or Lord) there could be no transition between the world and Brahman for one who is caught up in the world. The world of names and forms (*nāma-rūpa*) is ordinarily seen by us to be different from Brahman, and in order to free ourselves from it, we must affirm a spiritual ground (*adhiṣṭhāna*) for our experience and look upon the creative power that sustains and controls this experience as our own ideal mode of action. If one's view of the world is such that the world is taken as completely self-explanatory, self-sufficient, and real, then one would hardly be encouraged to seek a transcendence of it.

Whether seen as a theoretical necessity or as a practical requirement, Īśvara is thus taken by the Advaitin, from the standpoint of the phenomenal world, as the material and efficient cause of the world. "Those who think about creation (*sṛṣṭi*)," Śaṁkara writes, "think that creation is the expansion of Īśvara."[21] And the nature of this "expansion" is quite unlike anything that a Western (Judaeo-Christian) theologian would affirm. "The activity of the Lord," Śaṁkara maintains, ". . . may be supposed to be mere sport (*līlā*), proceeding from his own nature, without reference to any purpose."[22]

The concept of *līlā*, of play or sport, seeks to convey that Īśvara creates (sustains and destroys) worlds out of the sheer joy

21 Śaṁkara, Commentary on *Māṇḍūkya Kārikā*, I, 7, in *Select Passages from Śaṅkara's Commentary on Māṇḍūkya Upaniṣad and Kārikā*, trans. by T. M. P. Mahadevan (Madras: Ganesh & Co., 1961).

22 Śaṁkara, *Brahmasūtrabhāṣya*, II, 1, 33, trans. by George Thibaut, *op.cit.*

of doing so. Answering to no compelling necessity, his creative act is simply a release of energy for its own sake. Creation is not informed by any selfish motive. It is spontaneous, without any purpose. No moral consequences attach to the creator in his activity, for *līlā* is precisely different in kind from all action which yields results that are binding upon, and which determine, the actor. It is simply the Divine's nature to create just as it is man's nature to breathe in and out. *Līlā* thus removes all motive, purpose, and responsibility from Īśvara in his creative activity. Having no need to create and having no consequences attach to his action, Īśvara cannot be held responsible for the actions that arise subsequently within the fields of his creation. *Līlā* avoids thereby any problem of evil of the sort associated with Judaeo-Christian theism, and it sets aside as meaningless any question of why Īśvara creates in the first place. There can be no "why" to creation.

IV

Still *satkāryavāda* and Īśvara's sportive activity are true only phenomenally: they are negated in Brahman-experience where no distinction at all is perceived between cause and effect. *Satkāryavāda* thus prepares the way for the affirmation of *vivartavāda*, the theory that the effect is only an apparent manifestation of its cause.[23]

As pointed out before, Advaita is not alone in its adherence to *satkāryavāda*. The Sāṁkhya system likewise explains the cause-effect relation in its terms; but whereas the Sāṁkhya goes on to

23 Sarvajñātman, a tenth-century Advaitin, bears out this interpretation when writing, "In the Vedāntic view, the transformation theory is the preliminary step to the manifestation theory."—*Saṁkṣepa Sārīraka*, trans. by T. Mahadevan (unpublished MS, University of Madras, 1943).

Professor Olivier Lacombe makes this same point when he notes that "nous savons que pour comprendre le *vivartavāda* il faut avoir passé par l'etapé du *pariṇāmavāda*."—*L'Absolu selon le Vedānta* (Paris: P. Geuthner, 1937), p. 237.

assume that the effect not only pre-exists in the cause but is an actual transformation (*pariṇāma*) of it, Advaita argues that the effect is nothing but an apparent manifestation of the cause, that "A thing is not rendered as being a thing having parts, merely by imagining through Nescience (Avidyā) that it has different aspects. The moon, for instance, does not in fact become more than one, merely because she appears to be more than one, to an eye affected by double vision."[24]

That which is One cannot in reality become Many, it can only appear to be Many—and this through superimposition grounded in our ignorance. If the cause (Brahman) actually transformed itself into an effect different from it (the phenomenal world *qua* phenomenal world), then the effect would still have an independent reality in that there would be a metaphysical basis for some kind of distinction between them.[25] But Brahman, the "cause," is alone Real; hence, "an effect is merely a name made current by speech."[26] And thus

> Brahma appears to become susceptible of (i.e., appears to be the basis of) all phenomenal behaviour by way of modifications etc., by reason of the distinctions of aspects or forms characterized by names and forms imagined through Nescience . . . while in its truest nature Brahma subsists only in its unmodified aspect and is beyond all phenomenal behaviour . . . .[27]

V

In sum: for Advaita Vedānta, the creation or evolution of the world, as indeed the status of the world itself, is only an appar-

24 *Brahmasūtrabhāṣya*, II, 1, 27, trans. by V. M. Apte, *op.cit.*

25 Appaya Dīkṣita, a sixteenth-century Advaitin, writes: "That change, which is of the same grade of reality as the thing, is transformation [*pariṇāma*]; what is not of the same grade of reality is illusory manifestation [*vivarta*] . . . ."—*Siddhāntaleśasaṅgraha*, as quoted by T. M. P. Mahadevan in *The Philosophy of Advaita* (Madras: Ganesh & Co., 1957), p. 193.

26 *Brahmasūtrabhāṣya*, II, 1, 14, trans. by V. M. Apte, *op.cit.*

27 *Ibid.*, II, 1, 27.

ent truth. Creation may be considered a positive activity of Brahman only from the *vyavahārika* or empirical point of view; only to the extent that we are subject to *māyā*, *avidyā*, and are engaged in the activities of *adhyāsa*. When in this condition one attempts to understand the relation between Brahman and the world, one is compelled rationally to uphold creation in terms of *satkāryavāda*—the theory that the effect pre-exists in its cause—that Brahman is the material and efficient cause of the world. Further, when seen from this standpoint and in terms of the requirements of spiritual experience, Brahman becomes Īśvara, the creative Lord who calls forth worlds, maintains them, and re-absorbs them as *līlā*, as sport or play. Īśvara's distinctive activity is thus an outpouring of energy for its own sake. There is no purpose to creation, as Īśvara has no need that is to be fulfilled in creation. He is a free, unlimited power.

But having arrived at all of this within *māyā*, one cannot ascribe ultimacy to it. Creation is only apparent change, it is not a modification of Brahman in reality, and hence *vivartavāda*. From the standpoint of Brahman-experience, from the standpoint of Brahman itself, there is no creation: Reality is non-dual.

The whole import of *vivartavāda* then is to bring the mind away from its involvement in *māyā*, away from the need to ask the question about the relation between Brahman and the world, the asking of which implies the recognition of the world as a separate entity, to its experiencing directly the Reality that is Brahman. The world is first affirmed as an empirical reality, an affirmation which, apart from its inherent philosophical justification, avoids a subjective idealism that would overcome duality without self-transcendence; and secondly as an "effect" of Brahman which again, apart from its logical justification, has the practical value of bringing the mind that is attached to the world into an awareness of Brahman as its cause. *Vivartavāda* then affirms the appearance-only status of the effect and thus points the way to the subration of the world in

Brahman through "de-superimposition" (*apavāda*), through the reducing of effects back into their causes.[28] This leads the mind to Brahman, to Reality, where all questions of the relation between it and something else are silenced.

VI

Can this Advaitic analysis of the relation between Brahman and the world be vindicated? Is it a valid or fruitful philosophical analysis?

The answer, we believe, is yes—provided that one is willing to acknowledge that the problem to which the analysis is directed is a legitimate philosophical problem and not a piece of verbal nonsense. And in order to acknowledge that it is a genuine philosophical problem, one has either to affirm Brahman for himself as the sole Reality or accept such an affirmation as meaningful on the part of one who puts forward the claim that a non-dual spiritual experience is possible. If one acknowledges then that the problem —What is the relation that obtains between Brahman and the world?—is genuine, one must, it would seem, accept in large measure the Advaitic treatment of it.

The doctrine of *māyā* explicitly places the world of our ordinary experience where, ontologically speaking ,with the affirmation of Brahman, it properly belongs. If Brahman is Reality, then clearly the world cannot itself be fully real; rather it must have only a provisional status that is ultimately inexplicable. The world cannot be explained in itself, for the mind that would explain it is part of, and is conditioned by, that which is to be explained; it cannot be explained with reference to Brahman, for no relations can be established between them. The world appears to us in *māyā*; it disappears when we attain Brahman. The ultimate "why" of the

28 See Chapter VIII on *Mokṣa and Jñāna-Yoga*.

world cannot then be grasped. The world can be made intelligible only by employing an epistemological category of *avidyā*. And seeing its specific function in human consciousness as *adhyāsa*, as superimposition, does make sense of this our worldly misperception. Although a close description of this process in terms of a detailed psychological analysis is somewhat wanting, the general characterization of the process of false attribution is persuasive: it is readily testable in experience.

As for the general doctrine of causation, apart now from any question about the relative practical efficacy of various theories, the *vivartavāda* is more convincing than the *satkāryavāda*, which is preliminary to it. This is because the general notion of causation implicit in the problem/solution is quite primitive. No clear distinction is recognized between a rationalist's concept of causation as necessitation and an empiricist's concept of causation as the observation of regular sequences under various specifiable conditions. If causation were understood "empirically," rathen than, "rationally," as a kind of heuristic principle that enables us to discover special relations among events that admit of prediction, many of the controversies between the *satkāryavāda* and the *asatkāryavāda* (e.g., whether it is possible for any given effect to issue from any cause) would disappear.

Further, the appeal to Īśvara in this context is somewhat problematic. Theoretically, it would seem that the doctrine of *māyā* as a "concealing" and "distorting" power can account for Appearance, as far as it can be accounted for, without the need for Īśvara as an explanatory concept; and especially since it is maintained that the "existence" of Īśvara as such cannot be demonstrated rationally. Īśvara, according to Advaita Vedānta, can be affirmed only on the grounds of experience, as a content of experience (as *saguṇa* Brahman, the harmonization of distinctions), or as a necessary condition for spiritual experience. Once so affirmed, however,

Īśvara's creative activity is properly seen as *līlā*, as a free, sportive activity. If it were seen otherwise, it would lead to the kind of irresolvable dualism that has so often dogged the course of Western theology. Logically, as pointed out by many a philosopher, one simply cannot have the full reality of a transcendent God and the full reality of the world. One must have either a limited God (subordinate in some sense to the world) or an unlimited Reality and an "appearance-only" world. By conceiving of Īśvara's activity as *līlā*, the Advaitin is able to place Īśvara as well as the world under *māyā* and thereby retain the unqualified Reality of Brahman.

The final teaching of Advaita on causation—that no causal ralation can be established between Brahman and the world, in that the world as effect must be only an appearance of Brahman and not something put forward by it as a substantial reality—does seem to be sound. A spiritual monistic or non-dualistic philosophy must be a multi-leveled one in which the intellect is incapable of establishing either universal, necessary relations between these levels or repeatable, observable conjunctions between them. From the phenomenal standpoint, within which any such causal relation would be established, Brahman and the world are different in kind; qualitatively, they are incommensurable. In order to set forth a causal relation between two things, a minimum requirement is that they be of the same order of being. One cannot reason legitimately from an effect back to a cause when the effect is formed and the cause is formless, when the effect is time-bound and the cause is timeless, and so on. In short, one cannot establish relations between disparate levels of being: one can only trace the generation of these levels back to the thinking subject as it relates to the world and account for the manner in which they arise in terms of axiological and noetic considerations. And this is precisely what Advaita Vedānta does in its criterion of subration and in its doctrines of *māyā*, *avidyā*, and *adhyāsa*.

Assuming the meaningfulness of the notion of Brahman, the final teaching of *vivartavāda* would seem to be the correct answer to any question concerning the relation that obtains between Brahman, Reality, and the world of multiplicity, Appearance. It insures the non-dual character of Brahman and, although it does not actually explain the world in terms of the world, it shows how it makes its appearance in experience. What is a loss to strict intellectual satisfaction might nevertheless be a gain to that love of wisdom, which, after all, still has something to do with what we call philosophy.

4 The Self

Brahma satyaṁ jagan mithyā jīvo brahmaiva nā'paraḥ.
Brahman is real, the world is illusory, the self is not-different from Brahman.

The central concern of Advaita Vedānta is to establish the oneness of Reality and to lead the human being to a realization of it. Any difference in essence between man and Reality must be erroneous, for one who knows himself knows Reality, and this self-knowledge is a "saving" knowledge; it enables the knower to overcome all pain, misery, ignorance, and bondage. What, though, is the self, the knowledge of which yields freedom and wisdom? How does it relate to what we ordinarily take to be our self—our physical organization, our mental activities and capacities, our emotional and volitional life? These are the questions Advaita Vedānta is committed to answer; the answers being at the very core of Advaita philosophy.

I

Bāṣkali asked Bāhva three times about the nature of Brahman: the latter remained silent all the time, but finally replied:—I teach you, but you understand not: silence is the Ātman.[1]

A person's essence is unapproachable through his name; and in the Spirit, in the Absolute where pure silence reigns, all names are rejected.

1 Śaṁkara, *Brahmasūtrabhāṣya,* III, 2, 17.

The application of a label to someone too often implies that in the deepest ontological sense that someone is a "something." Lables are mere conventions and sounds; and to disown all labels in a penetrating inward intuition means not only to recognize the "nothing" that one is but also to become the silence, the "everything" that alone is.

Ātman (or *paramātman*, the highest Self), for Advaita Vedānta, is that pure, undifferentiated self-shining consciousness, timeless, spaceless, and unthinkable, that is not-different from Brahman and that underlies and supports the individual human person.

Ātman is pure, undifferentiated, self-shining consciousness: It is a supreme power of awareness, transcendent to ordinary sense-mental consciousness, aware only of the Oneness of being. Ātman is that state of conscious human being wherein the divisions of subject and object, which characterize ordinary consciousness, are overcome. Nothing can condition this transcendental state of consciousness: among those who have realized it, no doubts about it can arise. Ātman is thus void of differentiation, but for Advaita it is not simply a void: it is the infinite richness of spiritual being.

"This Ātman is self-luminous."[2]

Ātman is timeless: It cannot be said to have arisen in time, to be subject to a "present," or to have an end in time—for all such sayings apply only to what is relative and conditioned. Time, according to Advaita, is a category of the empirical or phenomenal world only. Time, with its before and after, can make no claim on the "eternal Now" which is the state of Ātman realization.

"This intelligent Self is without birth or death."[3]

Likewise it is spaceless: Spatial relations hold between objects of the empirical order; they cannot be extended to constrain that which is the content of spiritual experience.

2 *Bṛhad-āraṇyaka Upaniṣad,* IV, 3, 9.
3 *Kaṭha Upaniṣad,* I, 2, 18.

"It is impossible for the body to be the receptacle of the Self."[4]

And unthinkable: "The eye does not go there, nor speech, nor mind."[5]

"It is great and self-effulgent, and its form is unthinkable."[6]

Thought functions only with forms, in multiplicity; Ātman, being without determinate form and being ultimately simple, cannot be an object knowable by the mind, perceivable by the senses. Thought is a process; Ātman is a state of being. Thought objectifies, Ātman is the pure "subject" that underlies all subject/object distinctions. "The knowledge of the Ātman is self-revealed and is not dependent upon perception and other means of knowledge."[7]

It is not-different from Brahman: Identity judgments such as those expressed in the *mahāvākya* (great saying) *tat tvam asi*[8]—"thou art that"—are not, for the Advaitin, mere tautologies: they are the concrete representation of a movement of thought from one ontological level (of particularity) through another (of universality) to yet another (of unity), wherein the attainment of the latter negates the distinctions between the former. One begins with individual consciousness (*tvam*), passes on to universal consciousness (*tat*), and arrives at the pure consciousness that overcomes the separative reality of both the individual and the universal and that constitutes their ground.

Tat tvam asi means the affirmation of a common ground, viz., consciousness, to the individual and Brahman. The identity is obtained by stripping away the incompatible or contradictory elements of the "that" and "thou" and thereby arriving at their common elements or basis. According to the Advaitin, if we were to take the term "thou" strictly as the finite individual person and

4 Śaṁkara, Commentary on *Kaṭha Upaniṣad,* II, 2, 12.
5 *Kena Upaniṣad,* I, 3.
6 *Muṇḍaka Upaniṣad,* III, 1, 7.
7 Śaṁkara, *Brahmasūtrabhāṣya,* II, 3, 7.
8 *Chāndogya Upaniṣad,* VI, 8 ff.

the term "that" as a transcendent reality, then clearly an identity between them is meaningless; by definition they are two different things. But there is a "secondary sense" of the terms that discloses the proper meaning of the proposition. If the "thou" denotes the pure consciousness underlying human being and the "that," the pure consciousness, which is the ground of divine being, then a complete identity between them does indeed exist. The individual self, apart from all factors that differentiate it from pure consciousness, is the same as the divine, apart from its differentiating conditions. *Tat tvam asi*, according to Advaita, is a significant proposition provided that we deny the reality of the two terms as such and grasp their basic underlying identity.[9]

In the depth of my being, then, I am not-different from Reality: the depth of my being, which is not "mine," is Reality. Man, according to Advaita, is not just a conditioned being, so that if you were to strip away his desires, his mental activities, his emotions, and his ego, you would find a mere nothing; he is spirit, he is consciousness, he is free and timeless being.

Ātman cannot be an object of thought, and it cannot be arrived at as the conclusion of a rational argument. In order, however, to orient the mind towards it and to prepare the mind to accept it as a fact of experience, the Advaitin does proffer rational arguments, the most common of which is a sort of *cogito ergo sum* argument. Śaṁkara states that "to refute the Self is impossible, for he who tries to refute it is the Self."[10] No one, Śaṁkara maintains, can doubt the existence of Ātman, for the act of doubting implies the very being of the doubter who must thereby affirm his own existence. Vidyāraṇa expresses the argument thus:

> No one can doubt the fact of his own existence. Were one to do so, who could the doubter be?

9 Cf. Śaṁkara, *Brahmasūtrabhāṣya*, I, 1, 17, and IV, 1, 3.
10 Śaṁkara, *Brahmasūtrabhāṣya*, II, 3, 7.

> Only a deluded man could entertain the idea that he does not exist.[11]

The argument is not without its difficulties. A subtle and unsupported transition is made between the Ātman and the *jīva* (the individual conscious being) so that the argument does not so much prove the Ātman as it does the *jīva*—the *jīva*, which has the kind of self-consciousness described in, and presupposed by, the argument, and not the Ātman, which is pure consciousness. In other words, by establishing the self on the basis of the inability to deny the doubter who would deny the self, the self that is being established, apart from any other difficulty in the argument, is necessarily a qualified one; it is the self in waking consciousness who is aware of an "I" and who, as will be shown, is associated with a qualified reality, the *jīva*, and not with Ātman, the non-dual Reality.

II

> The individual soul is not directly the highest Ātman, because it is seen to be different on account of the upādhis [limiting adjuncts]; nor is it different from the Ātman, because it is the Ātman who has entered as the jīvātman in all the bodies. We may call the jīva as a mere reflection of the Ātman.[12]

The individual human person, the *jīva*, is a combination of reality and appearance. It is "reality" so far as Ātman is its ground; it is "appearance" so far as it is identified as finite, conditioned, relative. The individual self then is empirically real, for it is a datum of objective and subjective experience; but it is transcendentally unreal, for the self, in essence, is identical with the Absolute.

In attempting to understand the status of the *jīva*, Advaita Vedānta proffers two theories or metaphors, both of which as

11 *Pañcadaśī*, III, 23–24, trans. by Hari Prasad Shastri, *op.cit.*
12 Śaṁkara, *Brahmasūtrabhāṣya*, II, 3, 50, trans. by V. H. Date, *op cit.*

indicated above are suggested by Śaṁkara.[13] A common intent informs these two theories, but the differences between them are instructive. According to the first, which is called *pratibimba-vāda*, the theory of reflection (and which is associated primarily with the Vivaraṇa school of Advaita), the *jīva* is a reflection of Ātman on the mirror of *avidyā*, and as such it is not-different from Ātman in essence. Just as in everyday experience where we know that the face in the mirror is not really different from the face in front of it, that the face in the mirror does not have an independent life of its own, and yet we maintain a distinction between them, so the *jīva* reflected in "ignorance" is not really different from its prototype, the Self, and yet it continues to be a *jīva* until the mirror itself is removed. The *pratibimba*, the reflection, is actually as real as the *bimba*, the prototype, being in essence the same thing; the *pratibimba* is misjudged to be different only because it appears to be located elsewhere than the *bimba*. One attains the truth of non-difference, then, the moment one understands that one is a reflection of Ātman that only appears to be different from it, but is identical with it in reality.[14] And just as the reflection of a person in a body of water varies according to the state of the water, according as the water is calm or turbulent, clean or dirty, so the reflection of the Absolute varies according to the state of *avidyā* upon which it is reflected. The minds of men vary: some are more, some are less, under the influence of passion and desire; some are more, some are less, capable of intellectual discrimination and in-

13 Some interpreters of Advaita (e.g., V. P. Upadhyaya) have suggested that three theories to explain the non-dual status of the *jīva* and its phenomenal appearance are to be found in Advaitic literature: *the pratibimba-vāda*, the *avacchedavāda*, and the *ābhāsa-vāda* (of Sureśvara). The differences between the *pratibimba-vāda* and the *ābhāsa-vāda*, however, are extremely subtle, and were not emphasized to any very great extent in the literature as a whole.

14 Cf. B. K. SenGupta, *A Critique on the Vivaraṇa School* (Calcutta: S. N. SenGupta, 1959), pp. 240–41.

sight. The Absolute appears differently according to these differences among individuals.

The first description of, or metaphor about, the appearance of the *jīva* has this advantage; it suggests that the clearer the mirror, the more perfect is the relation between the *jīva* and Ātman. As the mirror loses its individual characteristics it reflects better what is presented to it. The *pratibimba-vāda* suggests, then, that rather than being restless, anticipating, and desiring, our minds ought to be like a clear and calm mirror capable of reflecting truth.

The second theory (which is associated with the Bhāmatī school of Advaita) is called *avaccheda-vāda*, the theory of limitation. According to this theory, consciousness that is pure and unqualified, without sensible qualities, cannot be "reflected," and hence the analogy with the mirror breaks down when pressed to the point to which the *pratibimba-vāda* takes it. The individual is not so much a reflection of consciousness as he is a limitation of it; a limitation that is constituted by the *upādhi* of ignorance. The term *upādhi*, translated usually as "limiting adjunct" or "limiting condition," is frequently employed in Advaitic analysis. A *upādhi* generally means the qualification or limitation of one thing by another thing. For Advaita, in the context with which we refer to it, a *upādhi* is the limitation, owing to mental imposition, of infinity by finitude, of unity by multiplicity. It results in the seeing of the Infinite by, and through, limitations or conditions that do not properly belong to the Infinite. As long as ignorance exists, the individual engages in *adhyāsa* (superimposition) and does not see himself as he really is, but as a being separated from other individuals, conditioned and finite. Just as space (*ākāśa*) is really one but is seen through limitations as if it were divided into particular spaces like the space in a pot or a room, so is the Self—it is one but is seen through limitations as if it were multiple. The limitations, grounded in ignorance, are only conceptual: the self is essentially unlimited and real.[15]

Avaccheda-vāda, the theory of limitation, gives a somewhat greater empirical reality to the *jīva* than does *pratibimba-vāda*, the theory of reflection, in this sense that, whereas the the *jīva* in the *pratibimba-vāda* is a mere fleeting image, as it were, the *jīva* in the *avaccheda-vāda* is a necessary "practical" reality. Because we are subject to *avidyā*, it is necessary, as a matter of practical convenience, that we perceive individual persons and objects as separate, distinct realities. For both theories, however, the *jīva qua jīva* is an illusory appearance. The existential status of the individual human person, whether as a reflection of Ātman or as a limitation of Ātman, is one of qualified reality; its essential status is that of unqualified reality, of identity with the Absolute. Whereas the world is "false" (*mithyā*), according to Advaita, in that it may completely disappear from consciousness when subrated, the self (*jīva*) is only misperceived: the self is really Brahman. In other words, the self is not so much denied by Brahman as its real nature (as not-different from Brahman) is revealed when Brahman is realized.

15 The objection frequently raised against this position is that it is impossible (unintelligible) for the *jīva* to be a limited appearance of Ātman and at the same time to be the locus of *avidyā*; for it becomes then both the product and the source of the limiting adjuncts. For purposes of understanding the Advaitic position on the nature of the *jīva's* status, however, it is not necessary to examine the complete dialectical interplay between these two rival theories, for the "theories" are in fact but metaphors and analogies that seek to clarify rather than to demonstrate the ultimate non-difference between the *jīva* and Ātman, and the phenomenal status of the *jīva* as *jīva*; and being metaphors, they cannot be pressed to the point where they can stand as independent theoretical statements. In other words, the Advaitin of whatever persuasion begins with the central experience of non-duality and looks for ways by which this can be communicated and for what follows from it; he does not arrive at the fact of non-duality as the conclusion of an inductive or deductive demonstration.

III

The analysis of the empirical or phenomenal self in Advaita Vedānta, as we reconstruct it, is primarily a "phenomenology" of consciousness. It is a description of the kinds of awareness that one has of oneself when one is subject to *avidyā*. Advaita does not so much explain the self as it describes the process by which we come to believe that it exists. In short, the Advaitic analysis of the empirical or qualified self is concerned to answer this question: By what process of mis-identification do we form the belief in the reality of what is in fact an illusory appearance?

The first domain of our self-awareness, according to Advaita, is that of our being awake in relation to a world of external objects. We take ourselves as "I" or "me" so far as we are aware of things, events, and processes. Waking consciousness (*jāgarita-sthāna*) or primitive I-consciousness is "intentional": Advaita agrees with existential phenomenology on this point that waking consciousness must have an object in order to be; that being awake means being *awake to*.[16] And this being awake is never static. Waking consciousness ceaselessly shifts its attentive energies to different objects and to different aspects of a single object; it lapses into disinterest and is freshly stimulated by other interests. Waking consciousness is thus time-bound: when in it we do not see things all at once; nor do we think about things in a comprehensive totality; we are constrained to a successive representation, to a considering of things one at a time.

According to the *Māṇḍūkya Upaniṣad*, wherein the analysis of the states of consciousness of the self is given, waking conscious-

16 Or as Sureśvara puts it: ". . . There is no manifestation of the 'I' without a modification of the mind directed to the external . . . ."—*Naiṣkarmya Siddhi*, III, 58, trans. by A. J. Alston, *op.cit.*

ness is directed towards the enjoyment of gross objects.[17] It is involved in desire and consequently is dissatisfied, for no object is capable of sustaining our interest in it; no object is capable of fulfilling the demands that we make upon it. We are aware of ourselves initially, then, as waking, time-bound, and enjoyment-seeking, but subsequently as dissatisfied beings. This self that is so dissatisfied, according to Advaita, is the self that has identified itself with its physical body. In waking consciousness we are aware that we are a part of physical nature, that we are formed from it, that we are sustained by it, and that eventually we return to it. The *Taittirīya Upaniṣad* speaks of this kind of identification as the *annamayakośa*, the "sheath" or "vesture" of food (matter).[18] In waking consciousness we think that "this physical body is me"; and we miss the eby the truth of the Self. The physical body (or what becomes termed the *sthūla-śarīra*, the gross body) cannot be the Self, for it is conditioned, temporal, finite.

The first stage in the development of self-awareness, or the starting point in the phenomenology of consciousness, is that of waking consciousness, the basic standpoint of all philosophy. Advaita is not concerned here to deal with waking consciousness functionally; it is not concerned, that is, to explain the manner of the functioning of waking consciousness in relation to its contents.

17 "The first quarter is Vaiśvānara [all beings] whose sphere of action is the waking state, whose consciousness relates to external things, and who possesses seven limbs and nineteen mouths, and who enjoys gross objects."—*Māṇḍūkya Upaniṣad*, 3. Śaṁkara, in his commentary on this attaches no importance to the seven limbs; he says that they are incorporated only for the purpose of completing the imagery of the Agnihotra sacrifice as set forth in *Chāndogya Upaniṣad* (V, 18, 2). The "nineteen mouths"—the five senses, the five organs of action, the five vital forces, and the fourfold division of the internal organ (*antaḥkāraṇa*)—though, are looked upon as the avenues by which we are led to and become enjoyers of, gross objects. They are psychophysical constituents of the self that bring the self into contact with external objects and that make possible its attachments to them.

Taittirīya Upaniṣad, II, 2.

Advaita is concerned only to identify waking consciousness and to point out the kind of self-identification that follows from it. In waking consciousness the self has forgotten itself. Whereas in reality the self is Ātman, pure "subject," here it takes itself as a mere object. It is some-thing among other things; it is "estranged" from the fullness of its being.

The second level or state of consciousness distinguished by Advaita is that of dream consciousness (*svapna–sthāna*).[19] It is the level of self that is inwardly cognitive of the impressions carried over from the waking state: it is the level of self that draws its sensuous and passional materials from past experience and in turn influences future experience within the waking state. The dream state is the state of fancy and wish-fulfillment and in function, if not in content, it may be equated with the "subconscious" of analytic psychology. Śaṁkara states that "after the cessation in sleep of the activities of the senses, (the individual) creates a subtle body of desires, and shapes his dreams according to the light of his own intellect."[20] The dream state is thus a natural extension of the waking state, but, as further pointed out by Śaṁkara, the waking state lasts until the knowledge of Brahman is attained while the dream state is subrated daily by waking life. In other words, the stuff of dreams, although rooted in the waking life, is not empirically real in the same sense as the content of waking life, for one recognizes it for what it is, namely, fancy and desire (the illusory existent).

Advaita Vedānta attaches a good deal of importance, however, to the phenomenology of dream consciousness in order to show the continuity of consciousness and the persistence of self-awareness throughout all states of consciousness. The independence of the subject of experience from its object is clearly exhibited in the

19 *Māṇḍūkya Upaniṣad* 4. See also *Bṛhad-āraṇyaka Upaniṣad,* IV, 3, 9–10.

20 Śaṁkara, *Brahmasūtrabhāṣya,* III, 2, 4.

dream state. No matter how deeply involved one is with the objects of dream, one retains an independence from them (as embodied in the judgment "I had a dream") and indeed a greater freedom with respect to them than is possible in waking consciousness. One can violate all the rules of spatial-temporal relationships that hold between empirical objects when one is in the dream state; and one can readily "transpose" one's emotional relations to these objects from one kind of past experience to another. But because one is involved in one's dream as well as being a witness to it, one is committing a fundamental mis-identification of oneself with the contents of one's quasi-liberated consciousness. These contents are called subtle elements (*tanmātras*): not only are they less gross than the objects of waking consciousness, but they also subtlely influence the whole fabric of waking consciousness, constituting as they do the material out of which so much of "personality" is formed. And it is precisely this subtle influence that makes it difficult for the *jīva* to know itself, to become fully aware of the forces that motivate it and that mold its attitudes and values. The contents of the dream state are elusive, and from the standpoint of the experiencer, they are largely involuntary: they present themselves without conscious control or selectivity. Further, so far as the waking state is intimately bound up in the dream state, it too is largely involuntary. A complete freedom to choose the contents of consciousness is thus denied the *jīva*. The Advaitin would agree with Spinoza that we think we are free when we are aware of our desires, but that in fact we are not free as we fail to understand the causes of these desires—which causes, for the Advaitin, are traceable to a root cause of *avidyā*.

According to the Vedānta, the three *kośas* or sheaths that are associated with the dream state of consciousness and that constitute the "subtle body" (*sūkṣma-śarīra*) of the self are the *prāṇamayakośa*, the sheath of "vitality," the *manomayakośa*, the sheath of "mind," and the *vijñānamayakośa*, the sheath of "understanding." The *prāṇamayakośa* is the self identified as a vital being. We identify ourselves initially not only as gross physical beings but also as animate beings. The *Taittirīya Upaniṣad* regards this vital aspect of our being as consisting of five breaths[21] that pervade the body and give power to the senses and to the organs of action[22] that likewise constitute this vesture of the self. Although the physiology here is no doubt crude, representing, as it does, only the most basic awareness of the nature of vitality, the analysis does point to a furthering of self-awareness in the direction of the true Self and to the kind of mis-self-identification that we make. It has been shown in modern psychology (namely, by Freud) that all of us believe that "death is what happens to the other person"; that we cannot imagine what it would mean for our own consciousness to cease; that we believe ourselves to be immortal. This belief is grounded in the *prāṇamayakośa* in our identifying ourselves as persistent vital beings. But there is no genuine, that is to say, spiritual, immortality for the *jīva qua jīva*: it is condemned to "existence," to phenomenal reality, until it realizes Ātman.

The *manomayakośa* and the *vijñānamayakośa* comprise the mental life of the self. They are made up respectively of *manas* and the five organs of perception, and *buddhi* and the five sense organs. A general distinction is made throughout Indian philosophy between two aspects—functions or domains—of mental life: that of *manas* or "sense-mind" and that of *buddhi* or "intellect." The precise meaning and role given to these two domains of mental life differ from system to system as well as in the different stages in the development of a single system, but a core of meaning common

21 Identified as the in-breath (*prāṇa*), the out-breath (*apāna*), the diffused breath ((*vyāna*), the body space (*ākāśa* = *samāna*), which is the "context" of the vital forces, and the support (*puccha* = *udāna*) for these functions.

22 Identified as speech, hand, foot, anus, and genital.

enough is present throughout. *Manas*, the sense-mind, is an instrument, sometimes taken as a sense organ itself, which assimilates and synthesizes sense impressions and thus enables the self to make contact with external objects. It is involved with these objects and consequently gives rise to the possessive "my" and "mine." *Manas*, however, is somewhat blind, lacking as it does a discriminating objectivity, and is thus referred to as a mental condition of doubt (*vikalpa*). *Manas* rushes out through the senses, as it were, toward the form of any object presented to it and assimilates that form to itself. It only furnishes the self with percepts that must be acted upon, transformed, and guided by a higher mental function. This is the work of the *buddhi*, the intellect or reason. The *buddhi* is an instrument of discrimination, a faculty of judgment; it determines our intellectual attitudes, fortifies our beliefs, and makes understanding possible. Whenever one is aware of oneself, then, as a rational being who is capable of intellectual insight and judgment, one is involved in this *vijñānamayakośa*. Both the *manomayakośa* and the *vijñānamayakośa* form the *antaḥkāraṇa* or "internal organ," which is the psychological expression for the totality of mental functions in waking-dream consciousness.

According to Advaita, all the mental activities of the self who identifies himself as a mental being are subject to a pervasive *avidyā*. No true self-knowledge is possible until Ātman is realized, until there is a fundamental change in consciousness. The empirical self, being a subject, cannot be an object to itself. All knowledge that takes place apart from Ātman is within the subject/object situation: the self as knower, within the context of the waking and dream states of consciousness, is a self that necessarily separates itself from the object of knowledge and hence always imposes something of itself upon the object. In short, with *manas* and *buddhi*, with the totality of mental functions, we may be self-possessed but never possessed by the Self.

The next stage of consciousness identified by Vedānta is that of deep sleep (*suṣupti*), which is characterized by a bliss (*ānanda*) that follows from the holding in abeyance of all distinctions.[23] Its *kośa* counterpart is the *ānandamayakośa* and is referred to as the *kāraṇa-śarīra*, the "causal body" of the self. Deep-sleep consciousness is not "transcendental consciousness," the spiritual consciousness in which oneness is obtained, but it is not to be construed as a void on that account.[24] Defined initially in negative terms as an absence of objects, of desires, and of activities, it is then described in positive terms as a state of joyous consciousness. It is, writes Śaṁkara, "an abundance of joy caused by the absence of the misery involved in the [usual] effort of the mind . . . ."[25] Deep-sleep consciousness is the self as unified and integrated; it is not so much an overcoming of the distinctions that make for activity and desire as it is (like *saguṇa* Brahman) a harmonization and a being a witness (*sākṣin*) to them. Distinctions, in other words, are not abolished here but are present in a kind of pure potentiality; and for this reason the *jīva* is said here to perceive pure *avidyā*, the cause or source of all distinctions. Further, deep-sleep consciousness with its counterpart self-identification, the *ānandamayakośa*, is also called "causal"; it is the ground for future actions: the various sheaths that are manifest in the waking and dream states are latent here ready to unfold as prompted by the effects of one's past experience (*karma*).[26]

23 *Māṇḍūkya Upaniṣad*, 5.

24 The Advaitin argues that in the state of deep sleep, consciousness is present, that deep sleep is a state of consciousness and not of non-consciousness, although there are no objects there with which it relates or interacts. And this is because upon returning to waking consciousness, one does affirm that "I had a wonderful sleep." If consciousness were absent altogether in that state, no memory affirmation of it would be possible. Consciousness, it is believed, thus persists even in the absence of all of the instruments of sense and cognitive experience.

25 Śaṁkara, Commentary on *Māṇḍūkya Upaniṣad*, I, 5.

26 Cf. Vidyāraṇa, *Pañcadaśī*, XI, 69–72.

Lastly, the *Māṇḍūkya Upaniṣad*, through a series of negations and affirmations, describes the pure state of consciousness associated with Ātman.

> They consider the fourth to be that which is not conscious of the internal world, nor conscious of the external world, nor conscious of both the worlds, nor a mass of consciousness, nor simple consciousness, nor unconsciousness; which is unseen, beyond empirical determination, beyond the grasp (of the mind) undemonstrable, unthinkable, indescribable; of the nature of consciousness alone wherein all phenomena cease, unchanging, peaceful and non-dual.[27]

This is transcendental consciousness (*turīya*—lit., "the fourth") the attainment of which leads to self-realization, to freedom (*mokṣa*).

In later Advaita, as we have noted earlier, a distinction is made between two types or kinds of spiritual experience related to transcendental consciousness: that of *savikalpa samādhi*, the borderline experience, as it were, between the *jīvātman* and the *paramātman*; and that of *nirvikalpa samādhi*, the pure experience of Reality. The distinction between the two is subtle but important because it brings out so clearly the uncompromising non-duality of Advaita Vedānta and because it makes clear, in terms of the distinction between *savikalpa samādhi* and *suṣupti*, the deep-sleep state, the fundamental difference between Ātman and the *jīva*—from the standpoint of the *jīva*.

Savikalpa samādhi means "determinate" spiritual experience. In it an awareness of duality is absent, but unlike in *suṣupti*, the deep-sleep state, the emphasis here is not so much on the *absence of duality* as it is on the *presence of non-duality*. Whereas in *suṣupti* the self is still a knowing subject, although there is nothing there as such to be known, in *savikalpa samādhi* the self is aware only of the presence of Reality. In *suṣupti* all the phenomenal activities of the

27 *Māṇḍūkya Upaniṣad*, 6.

self are suspended in a kind of serene blank; in *savikalpa samādhi* they are concentrated on the Real. In *suṣupti* the self is still very much the *jīva*; in *savikalpa samādhi* the self is passing into Ātman.[28]

Nirvikalpa samādhi is the consummation of the process. It is the pure "indeterminate" intuition of non-duality. In *savikalpa samādhi* the self is aware of Reality; in *nirvikalpa samādhi* it is Reality.

IV

To sum up: the Advaitic analysis of the self into four states of consciousness shows that there is no discontinuity of consciousness, that there is but one consciousness, namely, that associated with Ātman, which appears in different states because of various *upādhis* or mis-identifications of self with one or more aspects of phenomenal selfhood. The four states of consciousness, then, are really stages in the development of one's power of awareness and are brought into correspondence with the ontological levels recognized by Advaita. The waking and dream states, which can be brought together under a single category,[29] correspond to the phenomenal world of gross and subtle bodies (termed in this context *Virāt* and *Hiraṇyagarbha*); the state of deep sleep and of *savikalpa samādhi* to the qualified Brahman (*saguṇa*) or the Divine (Īśvara); and transcendental consciousness, *turīya, nirvikalpa samādhi*, to *nirguṇa* Brahman or Reality.

28 Still, "even the view that the self becomes Brahman is only a verbal statement for he is always Brahman."—Śaṁkara, Commentary on *Bṛhad-ārayaṇaka Upaniṣad*, IV, 4, 6.

29 This bringing of waking and dream consciousness into a single category is justified by the manner in which relations are established between the various states of consciousness, by the fact that both are said to be comprised of the same "seven limbs" and "nineteen mouths" and by their ontological contexts, which together constitute the phenomenal world.

And just as the ontological levels form a hierarchy of existence and value—the final term of which is not so much a part of the series as it is an annulment of the series, being incommensurable with it—so the stages in the development of consciousness form a hierarchy, the last stage of which transcends and overrides all the others. In the waking-dream state the self is caught up with objects, external and internal, and loses sight of its true nature as pure "subject." In deep-sleep consciousness the self is free from objects but has not yet transcended itself. *Turīya*, the fourth, is that self-transcendence that brings about the awareness of one-self as not-different from Reality and the awareness of the finitude and ultimate lack of reality of what has preceded it.

Phenomenally, as *jīvas*, as individual conscious beings, we are multi-personalities. We become the roles and functions that we perform; we become the kinds of persons we conceive ourselves to be; we become the many identifications we form of aspects of our self. Although we recognize the forces and conditions that act upon us, social as well as physical and psychological, we remain their victims: we ascribe ultimacy to them because we know of nothing to take their place. This, according to Advaita Vedānta, is the process through which we come to believe in the independent reality of the individual self and, consequently, to deny the reality of the Self. Its root cause is *avidyā*, ignorance. We are ignorant so far as we make of our physical, our biophysical, and our mental and emotional vestures something substantial, real, and ultimately valuable—without realizing that all being, reality, and value are grounded in, and arise from, our true Self. We are ignorant so far as we take an expression of consciousness (waking, dream, or deep sleep) as constituting the highest development of consciousness—without realizing that our consciousness, being identical with the Absolute, knows no limit.

The Self is One, it is not different from Brahman. This is the central metareligious or metapsychological affirmation of Advaita Vedānta. It means that man is essentially spiritual; that in the most profound dimension of his being he is no longer the "individual" that he ordinarily takes himself to be, but that he is precisely Reality itself. The affirmation is based not on mere speculation, but upon experience supported by a phenomenological analysis of what we erroneously take to be our selves. For Advaita, to affirm oneself as Reality is an act of a free man. The knowledge of non-difference leads to freedom, to the realization of the potentialities of our human being.

5 Karma

According as one acts, according as one conducts himself, so does he become. The doer of good becomes good. The doer of evil becomes evil. One becomes virtuous by virtuous action, bad by bad action.[1]

Coarse and fine, many in number, The embodied one chooses forms according to his own qualities.[2]

According to the doctrine of *karma*, everyone—as a *jīva* in bondage to the world—is conditioned and determined by his conduct, as this is enacted over a period of innumerable births, deaths, and rebirths. Every deed that one performs has its effect in the world and forms within the doer a *saṁskāra* or *vāsanā* (tendency) that becomes the basis for his future deeds. *Karma* is thus a "law" that sets forth the relation that obtains between one's action as a *jīva* and one's state of being.[3]

1 *Bṛhad-āraṇyaka Upaniṣad,* IV, 4, 5, in *Thirteen Principal Upanishads,* trans. by R. E. Hume (London: Oxford University Press, 1931).

2 *Śvetāśvatara Upaniṣad,* V. 12, in *ibid.*

3 To the possible objection that *karma* denies freedom to man and is thus self-negating, M. Hiriyanna, a distinguished authority on Indian philosophy, writes: "To act with arbitrarily shifting motives would be to act from impulse, as many lower animals do. Hence freedom should be regarded as consisting not in unrestricted license, but in being determined by oneself. When therefore we ask whether belief in karma does not result in fatalism, all that we mean is whether it does or does not preclude self-determination. That it does not is evident, because the doctrine traces the causes which determine an action to the very individual that acts."—*The Essentials of Indian Philosophy* (London: George Allen & Unwin Ltd., 1949), p. 47. Hiriyanna then goes on to note the manner in which transmigration is involved in the *karma* doctrine. "Since, however, these causes cannot all be found within the narrow limits of a single life, it [the doctrine] postulates the theory of *saṁsāra* or the continued existence of the self (*jīva*) in a succession of

There is perhaps no other basic doctrine in Indian philosophy which has had such a hold upon the popular thinking and practical religion of India[4] and which, in spite of Plato's *Republic* and *Phaedo*, has met with as much resistance among Western philosophers, as the doctrine of *karma*. One reason for this is that Indian philosophy has failed to make explicit and clear just what the status of the idea of *karma* is. Indian philosophers,

lives. Thus the theory of transmigration is a necessary corollary to the doctrine of karma."—*Ibid.*

From now on when the term "*karma*" is used, it refers to the joint doctrine of the "law" of *karma*—the principle of causality which holds that all moral actions produce moral effects—and of *saṁsāra*—the principle that there is a transmigration of the self (the *sūkṣma-śarīra* or "subtle body") in a series of births, deaths, and rebirths.

4 It is difficult, if not impossible, to determine the precise source of *karma* in the Vedic tradition or the exact point in its development when it took hold. Some scholars (e.g., A. A. Macdonnell, Charles Eliot, and A. B. Keith) believe that it is essentially an un-Aryan idea, one which was taken over from Dravidian sources, while other scholars believe that it has its roots in the ancient *Ṛg Veda* itself. R. D. Ranade, for example, with Rudolph Roth, Otto Böthlingk, and Karl Friedrich Geldner, holds that an analysis of *Ṛg Veda*, I, 164, shows that "the three chief moments in the idea of Transmigration . . . are all implicitly found even so far back as the times of the *Ṛigveda*; and when these are coupled with the incipient idea of the quality of action (*dharma*) which determines a future existence, we see that there is no reason why we should persist in saying that the idea of Transmigration [or *karma*] is an un-Aryan idea . . . ."—*A Constructive Survey of Upaniṣadic Philosophy* [Poona: Oriental Book Agency, 1926], p. 152.

Another view that is widely held today is that *karma* is a Upaniṣadic extension of certain underlying beliefs that were prevalent in the early Vedic sacrificial period; namely, the belief that the performance of certain ritual actions automatically brings about certain results. *Karma* is just the extension into the moral sphere of the belief in the mechanical efficacy that governs the sacrifice.

Whether *karma* has its roots in the *Ṛg Veda*, or was borrowed from non-Aryan sources, or whether again it is but a natural extension of beliefs present in early Vedic times, is of historical importance. All the later systems of Indian thought agree, though, that *karma* is operative in life; they disagree only about *what* it is that transmigrates and about *how* it takes place; *that* it takes place is accepted, and this alone is of philosophical importance.

including Advaitic thinkers, in short, have neglected to approach the doctrine of *karma* critically. The purpose of this chapter is to show what the logical status of *karma* must in fact be within the metaphysical and epistemological framework of Advaita Vedānta and to indicate the position which it thereby occupies within the Advaita system. *Karma* is given a somewhat pronounced position here because of its importance in Indian thought and because it will enable us to explicate and apply integrally some of the basic epistemological teachings of Vedānta. Our contention is that for Advaita Vedānta *karma* is a "convenient fiction"; a theory that is undemonstrable but useful in interpreting experience.[5]

I

According to Indian philosophy, and especially as developed in the Nyāya system, a *pramāṇa* is a "means of valid knowledge." A *pramāṇa* is that which produces knowledge that is in accord with reality; it is that by which the subject knows an object.

Following the Bhāṭṭa school of Mīmāṁsā, Advaita Vedānta identifies six *pramāṇas* or "means of valid knowledge." These are *pratyakṣa* (perception), *upamāna* (comparison), *anupalabdhi* (non-cognition), *anumāna* (inference), *arthāpatti* (postulation), and *śabda* (testimony). To show the undemonstrability of *karma* within the framework of Advaita Vedānta, one has to show that *karma* cannot be secured by any of these *pramāṇas*; that *karma* cannot be established by any of the means of knowledge available to man.[6]

5 We are not suggesting that Śaṁkara or other members of the Advaita school explicitly hold that *karma* is a "convenient fiction" (they in fact tend to affirm *karma* without any such qualification); we were concerned only to show that from the metaphysical and epistemological framework of Advaita, the status of *karma* as a "convenient fiction" logically follows.

6 Śaṁkara refers only to *pratyakṣa, anumāna,* and *śabda* as *pramāṇas*; the later Advaitins accept the others as well.

In terms of *pratyakṣa* (perception), which is described by Vedānta as the going out of the *manas* (mind) or *anataḥkāraṇa* (internal organ) through the *indriyas* (senses) to the object and the assuming of its form, it is clear that *karma* cannot be established, simply because it is not an object like a table, a tree, or a pot that is available to immediate sense experience. *Pratyakṣa* yields knowledge of the qualities of an object (like its color, size, texture) and the relations that constitute it (e.g., the universal "tableness" in the perception of a table); it does not and cannot yield knowledge of law-like relations between objects in Nature.[7]

The same holds true of *upamāna* (comparison) and *anupalabdhi* (non-cognition), which respectively yield knowledge as derived from judgments of similarity (that a remembered object is like a perceived one) and from judgments of absence (that a specific object is non-existent at a given time and place). Judgments founded on *upamāna* are of the sort "Y is like X," where X is an object immediately perceived and Y is an object previously perceived and now brought to consciousness in the form of memory. Judgments founded, on *anupalabhi* are of the sort "There is no Z in this room," where Z is an object that would be perceived then and there if it did exist: neither is of the kind "The law of *karma* is operative in Nature." Although Advaita keeps these first three *pramāṇas* separate and distinct from each other, they do have this common element that their fundamental origin and locus is perceptual. Now to expand this somewhat in terms of empirical experience as a whole, it is generally recognized today that there is at least one requirement that a theory about an experience must satisfy if it can be empirically validated. One must be able to move (directly or indirectly through deduction) from the theory to the data of which it is about and determine by observation whether the theory

7 Cf. T. M. P. Mahadevan, *The Philosophy of Advaita* (Madras: Ganesh & Co., 1957), p. 19ff.

or hypothesis does bring the data together in a confirming way. According to this basic requirement, *karma* is undemonstrable. There is no way known to us whereby one can observe one's "previous life" and its effect upon one's "present life." One can, in principle, see if one's conduct determines one's being in one's "present life"; one can see whether one's actions do reverberate back into one's nature and condition one's personality: one cannot, however, as far as we know, see beyond this.[8] "As one acts, so one becomes" is, in principle, demonstrable within one's "present life": as a law that extends beyond one's "present life," however, it is undemonstrable; and to assert it in this form as a literal truth would involve an unjustified extrapolation from a limited phenomenal fact. In Kantian language, it would be extending a concept beyond experience.

The next *pramāṇa*, or source of valid knowledge, is that of *anumāna* or "inference"; and here attention must be called only to the fact that valid inferential knowledge is obtained for Advaita only when a knowledge is attained of the invariable relation (*vyāpti*) between what is inferred (*sādhya*) and the reason or basis (*hetu*) from which the inference is made. *Anumāna* is mediate knowledge

8 It is of course true that the *rāja-yogins* claim that "by bringing the residual tendencies (*saṁskāras*) into consciousness [through concentration] (*saṁyama*) the knowledge of previous lives (*pūrva-jāti*) is obtained" (*Yoga Sūtra*, III, 18); nevertheless, the Advaitin does not use this claim as a support for *karma*, and even if he did, he would be faced with the difficulty, similar to that of "parapsychology" in general, of establishing new empirical laws of nature on the basis of the "extrasensory" perceptual experience of a privileged few. Until such time as a direct apprehension of previous life-states is obtainable in such a way that it can serve as confirming data for *karma*, *karma* must clearly be held to be undemonstrated. And it must also be held to be undemonstrable so far as the ability to obtain this data would seem to require a different kind of person—biologically, physically—that the man we know today. When one asserts empirical undemonstrability, it is understood that one is concerned with man as he now is, and not with man as he may conceivably evolve.

based on the apprehension, which is experientially uncontradicted, of a universal agreement between two things. A valid inference requires an invariable concommitance between the major and middle terms. Now *karma* cannot be established by inference for the simple reason that the nature of inferential reasoning in Indian philosophy precludes the possibility of a universal law like the doctrine of *karma* being the conclusion of an inference. It might be the result of simple induction, but not of inference as such.[9]

Apart from the *pramāṇa* of inference, there is one further notion of rational demonstration implicit in Advaita Vedānta. An idea or doctrine may be regarded as demonstrated if it "coheres" with, or follows from, the basic metaphysical principles of Vedānta and if its denial involves consequences that are self-contradictory.[10] According to the Upaniṣadic philosophy, where *karma* (in the Brahmanic tradition) is first explicitly formulated, and as interpreted by Advaita, the superpersonal Oneness of being (Brahman) as it is in itself and as it is manifest as the ground of human being (Ātman) is alone fully real and is thus, as we have seen, the sole "truth." All other dimensions and interpretations of experience have only a relative or provisional existence and truth-value. And *karma*, according to this way of thinking, cannot be applied to this Oneness.

9 Advaita holds that the universal proposition, the *vyāpti*, must be the conclusion not of the inference, but of an induction by simple enumeration. Two things may be taken as universally related, on this model of induction, when in our experience there is no exception to their relatedness. And here it is clear that *karma* cannot even be a genuine *vyāpti*, for the consequences of moral action, as affecting the actor over a period of innumerable births, are largely unseen, and hence they cannot be seen to be in uncontradicted relatedness to the actions. Induction, and hence ultimately inference, for Advaita, depends on perception and can extend no further than drawing out the implications of the relations based on perception.

For further study of the classical Indian model of inference, see Karl H. Potter, *Presuppositions of India's Philosophies* (Englewood Cliffs, N.J.: Prentice-Hall, Inc., 1968), Chapter V.

10 Cf. Śaṁkara, *Brahmasūtrabhāṣya*, II, 1, 6, and II, 2, 10.

There is nothing within the state of being designated by "Brahman" or "Ātman" that admits of being subject to *karma*. In its true nature the self is eternal and hence is untouched by anything that pertains to the *jīva* or the empirical world of names and forms (*nāma-rūpa*).[11] *Karma*, then, is only a "relative" idea; and it does not follow from the real nature of being. Its necessity is not logically implied by the metaphysical principles of Advaita, and its denial does not lead to consequences that are self-contradictory.[12] *Karma*, therefore, when looked upon as a rational concept or idea as distinct from an empirical, scientific theory, is not demonstrated, and, within Advaita Vedānta, it is rationally undemonstrable.

Closely related to *anumāna*, yet separate from it according to Advaitic epistemology, is the *pramāṇa* known as *arthāpatti* (postulation); and according to some interpreters of Advaita, *karma* can be justified by this mode of knowledge. Dharmarāja, the author of a classic Advaitic treatise on epistemology, writes:

> *Arthāpatti* consists in the postulation, by a cognition which has to be made intelligible, of what will make (that) intelligible, . . . *e.g.*, since in the absence of eating at night, the fatness of one who does not eat by day is unintelligible, that kind of fatness is what is to be made intelligible; or else, since in the absence of eating by night there is unintelligibility . . . eating by night is what makes [that] intelligible.[13]

In other words, *arthāpatti* is the assuming or postulating of some fact in order to make another fact intelligible. In the example cited, apart from possible inadequacies in the physiology, if one

11 Cf. *Ibid.*, I, 2, 50.

12 An example of an idea that would be rationally demonstrated within the framework of Advaita might be the very statement that all truths other than Ātman-Brahman are necessarily partial, relative, and incomplete. This idea follows directly from the assertion of Brahman as the oneness that includes and transcends all sense-mental experience.

13 *Vedāntaparibhāṣā*, V, 1–2, trans. by S. S. Suryanarayana Sastri (Madras: Adyar Library, 1942).

observes that a man is fasting during the day but continues to gain weight (or does not lose weight), one must assume that he is eating at night, for there is no other way to reconcile fasting and the gaining of weight. In expositing *arthāpatti*, a modern Indian interpreter and critic of Vedānta states that "the assumption ... is justified and is a valid place of knowledge ... because the fact assumed is the *only* one that can explain," and that "all necessary and indispensable suppositions, such as ... the law of Karma necessary for explaining the otherwise inexplicable good and bad luck of persons ... are cases of Arthāpatti."[14]

But *karma* is not justified by this *pramāṇa*, for it does not fulfill the requirement of uniqueness. *Karma* is not the only possible supposition that accounts for the good and bad luck of persons (i.e., the differences in their moral, intellectual, and spiritual capacities) as indeed many others (e.g., divine predestination or naturalistic hereditary factors) have been put forward and have been capable of generating strong belief. *Karma* is thus not established by *arthāpatti*: it is not the only way by which inequalities can be made intelligible.

The last *pramāṇa* accepted by Advaita Vedānta is *śabda* or "testimony." It refers in general to the validity of one's accepting as true that information that one receives from a "reliable" person or expert. In Advaita, the term *śabda* is used primarily with respect to *śruti*, the Vedic scripture, and more specifically, to what is said in certain passages of the Upaniṣads. Again, without our tracing the historical and psychological complexities involved in this belief in the authority of the Veda, it is necessary to call attention only to certain central facts: that for Advaita, as well as for the other "orthodox" philosophical systems in India, the appeal to *śruti* is not without its qualifications; that the appeal itself is based ultimately

14 D. M. Datta, *The Six Ways of Knowing* (Calcutta: University of Calcutta, 1960), pp. 240–41; 246.

on accepting the insights obtained through spiritual experience. One need not read far in the orthodox philosophical literature before realizing that some curious principles of scriptural exigesis are used to support ideas that, in many cases, have little direct relation to the text. More often than not, the principle of looking for a "secondary meaning" of a statement, rather than accepting the primary or obvious one, is adopted and is used to harmonize the statement with one's own philosophical position. Further, it is the rare Advaitin indeed who would hold to a scriptural utterance if it directly contradicted empirical or rational experience.[15] Scriptural authority is derived from spiritual experience and is accepted only for those truths that transcend reason and the senses. It has been rightly pointed out that "For purposes of philosophy, we may generally substitute in place of faith in scriptures, spiritual experience."[16] And even here the acceptance of *śruti* is not so much a question of simply believing in it as it is of whether the acceptance is a means for the attaining of one's self-realization. Śaṁkara himself states that "The existence of such objects as scripture, etc., is due to empirical existence which is illusory. . . . Scripture [and the distinction between] teacher and taught is illusory and exists only as a means to the realization of Reality."[17]

In terms of spiritual experience an idea may be considered demonstrated or validated for Advaita only if, phenomenologically, it describes a content of that experience. The Upaniṣads, according to the Advaitic interpretation, make clear-cut distinctions between ignorance (*avidyā*) and spiritual knowledge (*vidyā*), relative or finite existence (*māyā*) and the fullness of being (*Brahman*), and bondage (*bandha*) and freedom (*mokṣa*). When one attains freedom

15 Cf. Śaṁkara, *Gītābhāṣya*, XVIII, 66 and *Bṛhadāraṇyakopaniṣadbhāṣya*, II, 1, 20.

16 Krishnachandra Bhattacharya, *Studies in Philosophy* (Calcutta: Progressive Publishers, 1956), Vol. I, p. 95.

17 Commentary on *Māṇḍūkya Kārikā*, IV, 73.

and intuitive insight or self-knowledge, *karma*, as well as all other aspects of phenomenal experience, disappears from consciousness and no longer applies as a truth of one's being.[18] For the Advaitin, spiritual experience is experience of unity or identity: one cannot experience sequential time—past, present, future—when one is in a state of being that transcends all categories of time (*nirvikalpa samādhi*; *turīya*). *Karma*, therefore, cannot be a content of spiritual experience.

Karma is undemonstrated, and for Advaita Vedānta it is undemonstrable; hence, logically it has the status of a "fiction."[19] It remains for us to determine its "convenience" or "usefulness" in interpreting human experience.

II

If we put ourselves in the place of the Upaniṣadic *gurus*, we can see that they were confronted with several practical-philosophical problems related to teaching their students the way to *mokṣa*, and that it was precisely these problems that gave rise philosophically to their acceptance of *karma*. The first problem was that of working out a definition or conception of *mokṣa* or freedom itself. In practically every Advaitic text *mokṣa* is defined initially in terms

18 In the Advaitic interpretation, the *jīvanmukta*, the man liberated in life, has completely destroyed all the accumulated actions done in the past that have not yet borne fruit. This is called *sañcita karma:* it is distinguished from *āgāmi karma*, actions to be performed in the future, and from *prārabdha karma*, actions done in the past that have already begun to bear fruit. *Prārabdha karma* can never be fully obliterated: for the *jīvanmukta*, however, it merely runs out of its course without affecting him. Cf. *Brahma-sūtra* III, 3, 27, and IV, 1, 15; and Commentary on *Bṛhad-āraṇyaka Upaniṣad*, I, 4, 7.

19 "Fiction," in this context, does not mean a concept or theory that is necessarily false; rather a concept or theory may be called a fiction when it is undemonstrable, when it is impossible to determine its truth or falsehood, or when, in the language of Advaita, it cannot be established by any of the *pramāṇas*.

of liberation from bondage (*bandha*), and one of the central concepts employed in the notion of bondage is that of *karma*. But what is the necessity, one may ask, of defining freedom in terms of a bondage grounded in *karma*? The Upaniṣadic answer seems to be that except for the very few to whom Advaita comes naturally, as it were, an awareness of being in bondage is necessary to inspire one to make the quest for freedom;[20] and that *karma* provides a ready means for instilling this awareness. *Karma* can be acknowledged with but little imagination to be operative in life: it is far easier to talk about, and convince another of, the lasting effect of his actions than it is, for instance, to talk about the binding nature of his ideas, concepts, and language. Everyone can become aware of motives based on desire that lead to acts and decisions that have moral consequences. *Karma* is thus employed for formulating a definition of bondage that is necessary for formulating a conception of freedom.

Closely related to this first problem, and of more specific concrete application, is the problem of moral preparation. The Upaniṣadic sages were aware that there are moral prerequisites to the study of philosophy. Purity of heart, self-control, renunciation of sensuous pleasures, and the like are important for one who aspires to enlightenment.[21] The second problem, then, was, How can men be persuaded to live a moral life? One of the best answers to this problem is *karma*. If men feel that a tremendous importance is attached to every moral act and decision, that whatever they do will yield results that have an influence on the entire nature of their being, now and in the future, they will think twice about leading anything other than a moral life. Salvation consists in enlighten-

20 "There, so long as the nature of salvation is not definitely ascertained specifically, in whom could any desire for that rise up."—Madhusūdana Sarasvati, *Vedāntakalpalatikā*, trans. by R. D. Karmarkar (Poona: Bhandarkar Oriental Research Institute, 1962), p. 13.

21 E.g., *Kaṭha Upaniṣad*, I, 2, 2.

ment; morality is helpful to enlightenment; he who acts otherwise is doomed to *saṁsāra*. Śaṁkara bears out this "convenient" interpretation when he states that "unless a person is aware of the existence of the self in a future life, he will not feel inclined to attain what is good in that life and avoid what is evil. For there is the example of the materialists."[22]

The sages of the Upaniṣads were also no doubt aware that there is an enormous distance that most persons must cover before they are even prepared to pursue a life of the spirit; and also that even if they were able to embark upon the spiritual quest, they still could end in any number and kind of failures. It just doesn't seem possible that one life is sufficient for most men to attain *mokṣa*. Many persons, no matter how hard they try, no matter how devoted they are to the quest, actually attain very little. How then, the *gurus* must have asked, can we avoid discouragement and retreat among our students? The doctrine of *karma* solves this difficulty very directly. No effort goes to waste. What one cannot attain in this life, one will attain, or be better prepared to attain, in another life.[23]

The last problem for which *karma* offers a solution is the one most frequently pointed to: the problem of inequality and evil, of why there are such great differences among men in spiritual and mental capacity or why men occupy such different places within the socioeconomic order. The doctrine of *karma* provides a useful (if not demonstrable) answer to this problem. The spiritual and intellectual differences between *jīvas* are the results of their conduct. The place in society that they occupy at any one time is the result of their past action. The student who is intellectually less gifted

22 Śaṁkara, Introduction to the *Bṛhad-āraṇyaka Upaniṣad*, in Vol. III of *The Upanishads*, trans. by Swami Nikhilananda (New York: Harper & Brothers, 1957).

23 E.g., the *Bhagavad Gītā*, VI, 37–44, which tells about what happens to the man who involuntarily falls away from the path of yoga.

than another has only to look to his own past and present conduct. Suffering, misfortune, and ignorance, it is believed, cannot be traced ultimately to anything outside of the conditions of individual human experience itself.

In sum: The law of *karma*, which occupies so important a place in Indian thought and which is central to the manner in which the supreme value of *mokṣa* or freedom is conceived, must, for the Advaitin, have the logical status of a convenient fiction. It cannot be established through any of the "valid means of knowledge" recognized by the system. *Pratyakṣa* (perception), *upamāna* (comparison), and *anupalabdhi* (non-cognition) have to do only with immediately perceived phenomena, and, quite clearly, a law which states that any act has determining consequences for the actor over a series of innumerable births and deaths cannot be the content of sense perception. *Anumāna* (inference), as conceived in the tradition, depends upon the recognition that a subject possesses a property which is pervaded by another property and hence can only draw out the implications of sense experience; *anumāna* cannot establish that *karma* is operative in Nature. *Arthāpatti* (postulation) likewise cannot be the means by which *karma* is obtained as knowledge, because *karma* is not the only or unique mode of possible explanation concerning the existence of inequalities in Nature, and *arthāpatti* demands precisely this singularity of explanation. Finally, *karma* cannot be obtained through *śabda* (testimony) or, for the Advaitin, through the acceptance of *śruti*, for *karma* is not a content of spiritual experience. But *karma* was nevertheless used by the Upaniṣadic teachers and taken over by later Advaitins, with the expectation that it would satisfy certain specific problems that arise within the context of a philosophical practice that aspires to the realization of self-knowledge and freedom.

6 Aspects of Advaitic Epistemology

In our discussion of *karma* we saw how Advaita Vedānta distinguishes six *pramāṇas* or means of valid knowledge. It is necessary now to examine the status of these *pramāṇas* and see how they relate to the broader epistemological issues that any system of philosophy must face.[1]

The Hierarchy of Knowledge

According to the *Muṇḍaka Upaniṣad* (I, 1, 4), "There are two kinds of knowledge (*vidyā*) to be attained, the higher (*parā*) and the lower (*aparā*)."[2] *Parāvidyā*, the higher knowledge, is knowledge of the Absolute (Brahman, Ātman); *aparāvidyā*, the lower knowledge, is knowledge of the world—of objects, events, means, ends, virtues, and vices. *Parāvidyā* has Reality as its content; *aparāvidyā*, the phenomenal world.

1 In recent times a great deal of work has been done on many of the technical aspects of Advaita epistemology. The functions of the various *pramāṇas*, the nature of "meaning" and of "error," etc., have been examined closely (see Bibliography). We will not be concerned here with many of these matters, for they properly come more within the framework of historical analysis and exposition than within a "reconstruction." Further, except in the later phases of the tradition, and even here to only a limited extent (e.g., with Dharmarāja in the seventeenth century), there is little awareness of epistemology as a distinct philosophical discipline. Śaṁkara does not treat the *pramāṇas* as a separate topic and does not even refer to all six of what for later Advaitins become the standard ones. Epistemological isues are interwoven with metaphysical problems in Advaita and, for our purpose, are best understood in terms of their broad philosophical implications.

2 In the *Muṇḍaka Upaniṣad* this passage is set forth more in the context of ritualistic than of epistemological concerns. The philosophical point being made, however, is quite apparent.

These two kinds of knowledge must be incommensurable; for, according to Advaita, the higher knowledge is *sui generis*: it is reached not through a progressive movement through the lower orders of knowledge, as if it were the final term of a series, but all at once, as it were, intuitively, immediately. *Parāvidyā*, by the nature of its content, possesses a unique quality of ultimacy that annuls any supposed ultimacy that might be attached to any other form or mode of knowledge (e.g., reason or the senses). Just as Brahman is not a reality among other realities but is so completely Reality that all other orders of being, when taken as independent or separate from Brahman, are condemned to *māyā*, so *parāvidyā* is not one form of knowledge among others but is so completely knowledge that it overrides and overcomes any pretension to "real" knowledge that may be put forward on behalf of any other type or kind of knowing. Consequently, *parāvidyā*, the higher knowledge, is self-certifying: no other form of lower knowledge, such as inference or perception, is capable either of demonstrating or of refuting it.

The main axiological distinction in Advaitic epistemology is thus between *parāvidyā* and *aparāvidyā*. From the standpoint of *parāvidyā*, all other forms of knowing or modes of knowledge are equally *aparāvidyā*. Once Brahman is realized, all other orders of knowledge are seen to be touched by *avidyā* or a root ignorance.

But until that spiritual wisdom, that vision of non-duality, is attained, the lower (hierarchy of) knowledge as knowledge holds good. As Śaṁkara puts it:

> ... Prior to the realization of Brahma as the Self of all, all transactions (of the phenomenal world) for the time being are real enough. ... As long as the truth of the one-ness of the Self is not realized, the knowledge that all these effects, ... as characterized by the means-of-proof, the thing to be known, and the fruit [of knowledge], are unreal, does not arise in anyone. ...[3]

3 *Brahmasūtrabhāṣya*, II, 1, 14, trans. by V. M. Apte, *op.cit.*

In short, there is no way open to the mind to deny logically the results of its own functioning; that is, to deny the reality of its own contents. Any attempt to demonstrate the falsity of all knowledge without reference to an eternal Absolute is doomed to failure, for the mind that would deny, say, its own logic, without reference to Brahman, must be committed in advance to the use of that logic and any denial would thus be self-contradictory.

It is important to recognize this subtlety, for it is very easy to misinterpret the consequences of the Advaitic affirmation of *parāvidyā* as a unique, self-certifying intuitive vision of non-duality. It does follow from this affirmation that all other forms of knowing, such as reasoning, are ultimately without value, but—and this is the crucial point—this affirmation holds only for the man who has attained this special knowledge, who has realized himself as identical with Brahman: it does not and cannot hold for the man who has not attained this spiritual understanding. For him, or for the phenomenal standpoint in general, perception, inference, and the fruits of all the *pramāṇas* are entirely justified as valid means of knowledge. And further, from the standpoint of *parāvidyā*, the *pramāṇas* are justified as practical means of knowledge; that is to say, they are valid provided that they do not claim ultimacy for themselves.

We have, then, in Advaita this special kind of hierarchy of knowledge: that the final goal of knowledge, namely, spiritual intuitive insight, once attained, relegates all other forms and types of knowledge to a lower knowledge—lower at least because none of them is capable of bringing one to a realization of Reality or is capable of either demonstrating or refuting Reality—but when unattained, insures (that is, does not disturb) the validity of the lower forms of knowledge when they are applied appropriately to their own phenomenal spheres. The *pramāṇas*, such as perception, inference, and comparison, are justified as valid means of knowledge as long as they do not have any pretensions to finality or ultimacy.

Parāvidyā as an Axio-noetic State of Being

> Śaunaka, a great householder, properly approached Aṅgiras [his teacher] and asked: "What is that, venerable one, which being known, all this becomes known?"[4]

And the answer given, in effect, is: Brahman is that which when known, all else is known.

But this does not mean that a knowledge of Brahman carries along with it a knowledge of particulars, of individual objects and their relations in past, present, or future time, for Brahman is incommensurable with the empirical world: the empirical world of multiplicity, according to the Advaitin, disappears from consciousness upon the attainment of the "oneness" that is Brahman. *Parāvidyā*, the higher knowledge of Brahman, is thus not some form of supernatural, magical knowledge about Nature. It does not provide one with any facts about the natural order that are not obtainable through the *pramāṇas*.[5] As Śaṁkara puts it: "... Knowledge ... only removes the false notion, it does not create anything."[6]

The "all else" that is known when Brahman is known, then, must necessarily mean "all else of value." In other words, when Brahman is realized, *nothing else needs to be known*. When the self has found itself at-one with Reality, there is nothing of real value that remains to be known.

4 *Muṇḍaka Upaniṣad*, I, 1, 3.

5 Cf. Commentary on *Bṛhad-āraṇyaka Upaniṣad*, II, i, 20, where Śaṁkara shows not only that "one means of knowledge does not contradict another," but that scriptural knowledge, or intuitive experience, cannot contradict the testimony of the senses or of reason when they are operating in their proper domains. "You cannot prove," he writes, "that fire is cold, or that the sun does not give heat, even by citing a hundred examples [from *śruti*], for the facts would already be known to be otherwise through another means of knowledge."—*The Bṛhad-āraṇyaka Upaniṣad: With the Commentary of Śankarācārya*, trans. by Swāmī Mādhavānanda (Mayavati, Almora: Advaita Ashrama, 1950).

6 Śaṁkara, *ibid.*, I, 4, 10.

The "Why" of Avidyā

From the standpoint of Brahman, of *parāvidyā*, as we have seen, all other orders of knowledge are touched with *avidyā* or "ignorance." *Avidyā*, with its close relationships to the concepts of *māyā* and *adhyāsa*, is the primary epistemological category of phenomenal experience.

> Even before knowing Brahman everybody, being Brahman, is really always identical with all, but ignorance superimposes on him the idea that he is not Brahman and not all . . . .[7]

But what, one may ask, is the ultimate "why" of *avidyā*? What is its ontological source? Why are we its victims in the first place?

The Advaitin's answer to these questions shows why they cannot be intelligibly asked. "Knowledge and ignorance," Śaṁkara writes, "cannot co-exist in the same individual, for they are contradictory like light and darkness."[8] Knowledge destroys ignorance, hence, from the standpoint of knowledge, there is no ignorance whose origin stands in question. And when in ignorance, one cannot establish a temporal origin to what is conceivable only in time (as Kant was later to show in Western philosophy) or describe the process by which this ignorance ontologically comes to be.

The Advaitin thus finds himself in *avidyā*; he seeks to understand its nature, to describe its operation, and to overcome it: he cannot tell us why it, or the mental processes which constitute it, is there in the first place. With respect to its ontological source, *avidyā* must necessarily be unintelligible.

7 *Ibid.*
8 *Ibid.*, III, 5, 1.

The Self-validity of Knowledge

The *pramāṇas*, as previously pointed out, are taken to be justified as valid means of knowledge by the Advaitin provided that they do not have pretensions to establishing any ultimate or final knowledge. All phenomenal knowledge obtained through the *pramāṇas*, therefore, is "true" and yet none of it is "true." The doctrine that supports more fully this apparent equivocation in terms is known as *svataḥprāmāṇyavāda*—the theory of the self-validity of all knowledge.

Along with the Mīmāṁsā school of Kumārila Bhaṭṭa (seventh century) the Advaitin argues first of all that all knowledge is intrinsically valid (*svataḥ prāmāṇya*) in that validity arises from the very conditions that make for knowledge in the first place; and second that only that knowledge or experience is ultimately valid which is not contradicted by any other knowledge or experience. All knowledge obtained through perception, inference, and the like is true as far as it goes, but it is only knowledge of Reality that is ultimately true, for it is never subrated by any other knowledge or experience.[9]

An idea is held to be true or valid, then, the moment it is entertained (in the context of the theory no distinction is made between "truth" and "validity"), and it retains its validity until it is contradicted in experience or is shown to be based on defective apprehension. For example, according to the theory, if under the conditions of normal light and good eyesight I see an object and judge it to be a table, I immediately and rightfully trust my judgment that the object is a table and that I may safely place a book or a glass upon it. Whenever a cognition arises or a judgment takes place, it generates assurance about its truth. The judgment may be mistaken, but this is learned only later (e.g., the book falls through

9 For a concise statement of this doctrine in classical Advaitic literature, see Dharmarāja's *Vedāntaparibhāṣā*, Chapter VII.

the "table"). *Svataḥprāmāṇyavāda* is thus a kind of perverse pragmatism. Instead of "truth" happening to an idea, it is "falsity" that happens. A cognition, in other words, is like the accused in court who is considered innocent until proven guilty; it is considered true until it is shown in experience to be false.

According to Vedāntins, *svataḥprāmāṇyavāda* is thus a "psychology of belief," and it involves a logical justification of the way in which we believe. Psychologically, the theory holds that a person actually does believe in the validity of any cognition as soon as it arises within him. The moment one perceives an object and judges it to be something, one assumes that one's judgment is correct; one does not engage in an elaborate reasoning process to sustain this judgment; rather one acts upon it immediately. Psychologically, then, we are predisposed to accept as valid all of our judgments unless we have some specific basis for doubt, and we are quite willing to conduct the affairs of life upon these judgments.

Logically this whole process of belief, according to the Vedāntins, is justified, for there is no place outside of the knowledge-acquiring process itself where we may look for a way to confirm a judgment. One can look for external conditions to falsify a judgment, but cognitions must be taken as self-luminous (*svaprakāśa*). If it were necessary to make a supporting inference to sustain the validity of one's cognition (as would be the case in any view that looked to external conditions as the means of validating, and not merely falsifying, a cognition), then one would be placed in the position of having to make an infinite number of such inferences, for each supporting inference would require another one, *ad infinitum*.[10] If, for example, someone were to hold (as do the chief opponents here of the Vedāntins, the Naiyāyikas) that truth consists of a correspondence between statement and reality, with the test of

10 Cf. Kumārila, *Śloka-vārttika*, II, 47, for the standard Mīmāṁsā arguments that are accepted by Advaita Vedānta.

truth being a valid inference supported by "fruitful activity," the Vedāntin would argue as follows: A judgment ("this is water") is not validated by an inference ("any object which has X set of qualities is water; this object has X set of qualities; therefore, this object is water") and a supporting experience ("I drink the water and find that it quenches my thirst), because the premises of the inference would have to be established by some other inference and the supporting experience would have to be shown to be conclusive (for certain needs and desires are satisfied by merely dreaming of the proper objects), and so on indefinitely. Inferences may be of help to one in removing some doubt that stands in the way of knowledge, but, once the cause for doubt is removed, knowledge is present with its inherent validity and with one's belief in the validity. In other words, we look for support for a judgment only when we are in doubt about it, and we are able to eliminate this doubt only when we are unable to find the kind of conditions that act in such a manner to falsify the judgment. There need be no test for truth because non-contradiction is the sole guarantee of validity.

Still, non-contradiction, while insuring the validity of the *pramāṇas*, also leads to their ultimate non-validity, for non-contradiction here does not so much mean an absence of logical self-contradiction (the chair is and is not in this room) as it means the impossibility of subration—the impossibility of rejecting something on the basis of other experience—and this applies ultimately only to Reality. All the contents of the *pramāṇas* may be subrated in principle; all the activities of a *pramāṇa* may be rejected by a qualitatively higher experience and insight.

Hence, a twofold theory of truth: all knowledge obtained through the *pramāṇas* is true, but none of it is ultimately true.

In any attempt by a Westerner to appraise this theory we must, I think, acknowledge first of all that we are apt to reject this theory (or at least feel that it is rather odd) because it goes against a deeply ingrained positivistic habit of our mind that, largely under the influence of science, holds to the "hypothetical" character of truth—that nothing (with the exception of analytic statements) is true unless it is shown to be such in experience. We think it the mark of an intelligent person if he approaches all ideas, percepts, and concepts with a certain wariness and tentativeness, that he look to experience to confirm or validate cognition, not merely to falsify what is otherwise held to be intrinsically true.

It also strikes us that *svataḥprāmāṇyavāda* in contrast to the "openness" of our approach would tend to stifle various kinds of inquiry or the motivation to undertake them, for one adhering to *svataḥprāmāṇyavāda* would remain blissfully content in one's knowledge as long as it was not rudely contradicted.

The Advaitin's answer to these criticisms, however, would be simple and direct. He would answer that *savataḥprāmāṇyavāda* does not rule out doubt or a suspension of belief, for doubt is not a judgment or cognition in itself; it is merely a questioning attitude of mind. One can, to be sure, have a "doubting cognition" ("I doubt if a man will land on Mars this year"), and this comes under the Advaitic theory of truth, for one accepts one's doubt as valid. One can have a doubting cognition, then, but one cannot meaningfully be in doubt about one's cognition—whether it be a doubting one or not.

A more forceful criticism, therefore, might be that by the Advaitic theory of truth one could never know if one's ideas were true, in any positive sense of the term; all that one can know is that they have not been shown to be false. In other words, for this theory there is nothing *positive* in the notion of truth. It is like St. Augustine's doctrine of evil in which evil is regarded as a privation of the good; only here in the Advaitic theory, falsehood seems to be supreme, with truth as a privation of it.

This conclusion is not only compatible with Advaita Vedānta but also necessary to its metaphysical position. As we indicated earlier the Advaitin is convinced that the activity of a *pramāṇa* can be contradicted by a qualitatively higher experience. The whole of perception and reason is negated the moment there is a dawning of the truth of Brahman. If Brahman alone is real, then clearly there cannot be another order of truth that subsists in some kind of finality. From the standpoint of Brahman, all other knowledge is false.

The difficulty, then, perhaps comes to this: that while the whole of perception and reason, etc., may properly be taken as valid until they are replaced by a higher experience or more profound insight, it does not follow that each act of perception and reason must be so taken. Any order of knowledge can be rendered inadequate by a more adequate and embracing order, and it seems reasonable to accept the lower order as valid prior to its being shown to be inadequate; but this does not mean that the same thing holds for the specific acts of knowledge within that order. What we are trying to suggest, in short, is that, on the one hand, *svataḥprāmāṇyavāda* may be justified when directed to perception and reason as generic forms of epistemic activity (that we rightly believe in the adequacy of our senses and reason until we learn otherwise) but that, on the other hand, it may not be justified when applied to specific perceptual judgments or cognitive acts. One should be able to speak (and no doubt more clearly) in terms of the *adequacy* of a means of knowledge (its limit and extent) and the *truth* or *falsity* of the statements that are generated out of the activity of any of the means of knowledge.

Perception as an Act of Involvement

Avidyā binds one to a limited order of phenomenal experience; and this limited order is the domain wherein the *pramāṇas* function.

It is interesting to observe in this connection how the Advaitic theory of perception supports this claim by showing that every act of perception brings something of the world into one's consciousness.

Perception (*pratyakṣa*) is that means of knowledge that is obtained through an immediate contact with external objects. According to Advaita Vedānta, perception takes place when the mind (*manas*, or the "internal organ"—*antaḥkāraṇa*), through the various senses, assimilates the form (the "physical gestalt" ?) of the object presented to, or selected by, it and appropriates it to itself. Perception requires a modification (*vṛtti*) of the mind, a change, so to speak, in its proper form after the form of the object; it requires an illumination of the object by the light of consciousness.

Now although this self-shining light of consciousness (which is called, in this context, the *sākṣin* or "witness") remains essentially untouched by what it illuminates, perceptual knowledge—at the level of the empirical self—is clearly a joint contribution of the self and the object.[11] The mind, for Advaita, does not simply receive stimuli or impressions passively, combine them into percepts, and manipulate them while retaining, in an unaltered form, its own structures (as if the mind were some kind of sensing-machine); rather the mind is active from the start in its relations with the object and takes upon itself something of the character of the object. For Advaita, to know an object perceptually (its color, size, texture, and the relations that inhere, as it were, in it) means to become that object and to have it become a part of one.

Consequently, the self, in that state of consciousness wherein perceptual experience takes place, is always involved with the world. To be awake means to be caught-up with forms and relations; it means to have the mind filled with objects and with the desires generated by its contact with these objects. Perceptual experience

11 Cf. Śaṁkara, Commentary on *Bṛhad-āraṇyaka Upaniṣad,* III, 4, 2.

not only illuminates an outer world *to* consciousness but also brings the changing world *into* consciousness; it involves the self in the world.

The Role of Reason

Among the six *pramāṇas* identified by Advaita, *anumāna*, inference, or reason in general, is of special philosophical importance; for the manner in which one takes the power (and limits) of reason influences fundamentally the manner in which one interprets the world.

The theory of inference in Indian philosophy generally differs from classical Western logic in many interesting ways, but especially in this, that it involves a kind of scientific method of induction as part and parcel of it and hence is never purely formal in character (e.g., the null class is not admitted in Indian logic; all terms of an argument must have members). Inference, for Advaita, is thus an empirical *pramāṇa*: its task, as we have pointed out earlier, is to draw out the implications of sense-experience. And in doing this the inference is necessarily limited or relative in that every *vyāpti* or invariable relation between what is inferred and the cause from which the inference is made has a probability factor attached to it. The universal proposition is accepted as true as long as it "works," as long as no single crucial experiment or observation falsifies it; but there is always the possibility, in principle, that a future observation will falsify it. No rational necessity is attached, then, to any universal proposition or scientific hypothesis.

Similarly, the basic guiding principles that inform this *pramāṇa*, such as "causality," bear no rational necessity: they are, for Vedānta, essentially "heuristic"; they are accepted in order to enable us to organize perceptual facts, to predict sequences of events, and to guide us in our search for new facts and relations.

Anumāna produces knowledge that is relative to the extent, and kind, of human experience reflected in it and is thus always subject to correction.

There is one other form of reasoning closely associated with *anumāna* in Indian logic that is called *tarka*. Generally, it means a hypothetical argument; an argument that is put forth to prove something which, by its nature, is not amenable to direct proof by inference, but about which there is some basis to assert the conclusion.[12] According to Advaita, *tarka* is not a *pramāṇa*, a means to valid empirical knowledge, because there is no way by which the truth or falsehood can be tested of what is arrived at through *tarka*. *Tarka* arises from the rational imagination of individual men and is always subject to counter argument. As Śaṁkara expresses it: "There being no hindrance to human imagination mere reasoning [*tarka*] cannot be depended upon in matters which must be understood in the light of Śruti statements alone. The thoughts of some clever men are pointed out as fallacies by some other clever persons; while the thoughts of these latter too are turned down by some others cleverer still."[13] There is in short no finality to what is arrived at by *tarka*.

What then is the role of reason in Advaita Vedānta? As already shown, Advaita does accept *anumāna* as an empirical *pramāṇa*: reason is justified as an instrument by which we are able to understand and explain our empirical experience. Further, reason may be used to support the truths of spiritual experience in the form of "analogical reasoning" (*sāmānyatodṛṣṭānumāna*); that is, reasoning that is based upon analogies between the transcendental

12 This type of argument was developed most extensively by the Nyāya school of Indian philosophy and was used mainly for purposes of showing the absurdity of the contradiction of one's thesis; e.g., "If God did not create the world, then there would be an effect without a cause, which is absurd."

13 Śaṁkara, *Brahmasūtrabhāṣya,* II, 1, 11, trans. by V. H. Date, *op.cit.*

and the empirical orders of being. Analogies do not demonstrate anything; they may, however, provide the mind with some understanding, drawn from its own experience, of the nature of that which transcends empirical experience. Advaitic literature is replete with analogies and with elaborate analyses of them. They function not so much as a means of *convincing* one in any shallow rationalistic sense but as a means of *awakening* one to new possibilities of experience. As Śaṁkara puts it:

> [If *Śruti*] shows that reasoning also is to be allowed its place ... [this] must not deceitfully be taken as enjoining bare independent ratiocination, but must be understood to represent reasoning as a subordinate auxiliary of intuitional knowledge.[14]

In its epistemology, Advaita Vedānta is like a phenomenological art. Its main concern is to describe the primary moments of spiritual experience and to lead the mind to it. Reason is of value in enabling one to function in the world; and it is of greatest value when it enables one to transcend oneself and acquire thereby immediate understanding.

Advaita's "Realistic" Epistemology

It was pointed out earlier that Śaṁkara and most of his followers reject a "subjective idealistic" interpretation of the doctrine of *māyā* (that the objects of experience can be reduced, ontologically, to the knowing/perceiving subject) and insist upon the separation of the subject and the object *within the phenomenal world*. When translated into epistemological terms, this rejection of subjective idealism becomes the affirmation of a special kind of "realistic" epistemology.

It is rather curious that this aspect of classical Advaita has been overlooked frequently by Western students of Indian thought.

14 *Ibid.*, II, 1, 6, trans. by George Thibaut, *op.cit.*

In our rush to read Vedānta as an extension of either the Hegelian or Berkeleyan idealistic traditions, we fail to appreciate its distinctive character. For Advaita, "oneness" holds only on the level of Brahman-experience and must never be confounded with the world of multiplicity (the world of *nāma-rūpa*—names and forms). Any confusion between the two is precisely the basic characteristic of that false superimposition (*adhyāsa*), which is ignorance (*avidyā*).

Every act of knowledge that is obtained through the *pramāṇas* presupposes, according to Advaita, a distinction between the knower (*pramātṛ*) and the object known (*viṣaya*). Śaṁkara puts it in the most explicit terms: "An object is perceived by an act of the subject. The object is one thing, and the subject another. . . ."[15] As suggested previously, the arguments that are used to support this "realism" are usually put forward in the context of Vedānta's rejection of the Buddhist school of *vijñānavāda*.

Among the most important arguments that Śaṁkara uses is one that is essentially phenomenological. He simply appeals to what one must admit to be a fact of consciousness.

> The non-existence of external things cannot be maintained because we are conscious of external things. In every act of perception we are conscious of some external thing corresponding to the idea, whether it be a post or a wall or a piece of cloth or a jar, and that of which we are conscious cannot but exist. . . . [Thus] That the outward thing exists apart from consciousness, has necessarily to be accepted on the ground of the nature of consciousness itself. Nobody when perceiving a post or a wall is conscious of his perception only, but all men are conscious of posts and walls and the like as objects of their perceptions. That such is the consciousness of all men, appears also from the fact that even those who contest the existence of external things bear witness to their existence when they say that what is an internal object of cognition appears like something external. . . . If they

15 Commentary on *Bṛhad-āraṇyaka Upaniṣad,* IV, 4, 6.

did not themselves at the bottom acknowledge the existence of the external world, how could they use the expression "like something external?" ... If we accept the truth as given to us in our consciousness, we must admit that the object of perception appears to us as something external, not like something external.[16]

The separation of subject and object in all noetic experience is thus, according to Śaṁkara, an undeniable fact of experience. The moment the "I" appears as a subject, there is no way open to him to deny the conditions that give rise to his being an "I"—namely, a sense of separation between himself and a world of external objects. Further, according to Advaita, it is the functioning of our consciousness in relation to an external work that alone provides warrant for asserting possibilities and impossibilities in experience.

... The possibility or impossibility of things [their existence and the qualities they possess] is to be determined only on the ground of the operation or non-operation of the means of right knowledge. ... [The] operation and non-operation of the means of right knowledge are not to be made dependent on preconceived possibilities or impossibilities. Possible is whatever is apprehended by perception or some other means of proof; impossible is what is not so apprehended.[17]

And the nature of the perceptual process discloses that thing and idea are necessarily distinct.

Nor, again, does the non-existence of objects follow from the fact of the ideas having the same form as the objects; for if there were no objects the ideas could not have the form of the objects, and the objects are actually apprehended as external.—For the same reason (i.e., because the distinction of thing and idea is given in consciousness) the invariable concomitance of idea and thing has to be considered as proving only that the

16 *Brahmasūtrabhāṣya*, II, 2, 28, trans. by George Thibaut, *op.cit.*
17 *Ibid.*

thing constitutes the means of the idea, not that the two are identical.[18]

In the above, and in other arguments, Śaṁkara is clearly concerned to uphold a distinction between subject and object as operative in the phenomenal world. And in the light of the basic metaphysical principles of Advaita, this position and the arguments used to support it seem to be sound. There is, we must admit, something inexplicable in the very foundations of our situation of "knowers" in an empirical world. "To know" requires self-consciousness—the operation of a form-perceiving and form-making intellect that is time-bound and never capable of exhausting the possibilities of experience. The self cannot, on this level of its being, ever fully grasp itself as a subject apart from objects or objects apart from the self as subject. The two are mutually involved. When a distinction between subject and object is a necessary condition for some*one* to know some*thing*, then, there is no way in which one can, without self-contradiction, deny either the subject or the object. What is peculiar about this "soft realism" of Advaita is, of course, that the knowledge so obtained within the *necessary* dualistic structure of empirical knowledge is permeated with *avidyā*. A realistic epistemology is thus philosophically necessary but ultimately false. It is restricted to only a portion of human experience.

18 *Ibid.*

7 Advaitic Ethics

The criticism is often raised against Indian philosophy in general, and Advaita Vedānta in particular, that it turns its back on all theoretical and practical considerations of morality and, if not unethical, is at least "a-ethical" in character. If by "ethics" one means a rigorous, independent inquiry into problems of, and questions concerning, the meaning of value, the justification of judgments, and the analysis of moral concepts and concrete existential modes of behavior, then this criticism is justified. It is true that Advaita Vedānta, whether in its ancient beginnings or in its more systematic philosophical form, does not raise, let alone answer, many of what Western philosophers consider to be the most basic ethical questions.

The reason for this is twofold. First, the entire Advaita system is permeated with value questions, and in such a way, that an independent, separate treatment of them is unnecessary. Value questions do enter, however implicitly, into every ontological and epistemological analysis. For instance, in the treatment of the fundamental distinction between orders of being, the criterion used to establish these orders, as we have seen, is at once axiological and epistemological. The same can be said for the self and its modes of knowing. The levels of consciousness leading to Ātman and the hierarchy of *pramāṇas* culminating in *parāvidyā* are based more on value discriminations than on logical or ontological priorities. In Advaita few separate ethical questions are raised, for they are present in the manner in which Advaita raises and treats every metaphysical or epistemological question.

Second, in terms of actual human behavior and the manner of judging it, the neglect of ethics is quite purposive. The neglect is based on the belief that Brahman transcends all moral distinctions and that man, being essentially not-different from Brahman, is likewise in his essence "beyond good and evil." In the *Kaṭha Upaniṣad* (I, 2, 14) the demand is made: "Tell me that which you see as different from righteousness (*dharma*) and different from unrighteousness (*adharma*)." And in the *Muṇḍaka Upaniṣad* (III, 1, 3) an answer is given that "When the seer sees ... the source of Brahmā, then the illumined one completely shakes off both virtue and vice (*puṇyapāpe vidhūya*)." For Advaita, then, which insists on the sole reality of a distinctionless Oneness, there cannot be any absolute moral laws, principles, or duties. "Morality," if it has any enduring spiritual meaning, is simply a quality of the man who realizes his self as "not-different" from Brahman.

Like all other areas of Advaita philosophy, however, this morality is regarded, and its attainment is set forth, from the different standpoints that correspond to the various levels of human experience. The Advaitin does hold that one who has not yet attained self-realization is very much bound up in the moral consequences of his action: he is subject to ethical judgment, and he must accept a scale of values by which his own judgment may be informed.[1]

The most basic criterion for moral judgment recommended by Advaita is that those acts, desires, and thoughts that lead the moral

1 This practical side of ethics is largely taken over within Hinduism by the *āśramadharma*, the duties belonging to the various stages of life as set forth in the *Dharmaśāstras*. Advaita Vedānta does accept these, albeit as limited in application to one who has not yet fulfilled the Advaitic discipline of self-knowledge (*jñāna-yoga*). The Advaitin does uphold, in other words, the necessity for most persons to conform to the complex laws of conduct as set forth by tradition and as proven necessary for the welfare of the individual and society.

For purposes of our reconstruction of Advaita Vedānta, however, we set aside this traditional practical ethics. Advaita does not proffer any unique or special justification for it, and qualifies its acceptance of it with the understanding that it has only a possible instrumental value for one who is seeking freedom (*mokṣa*) and that it has no meaning at all for one who has attained this freedom.

agent to the highest good, namely, self-realization, are "good" and that those that lead him towards the fulfillment of egoistic desire, so far as they prevent self-realization, are "bad." According to the *Kaṭha Upaniṣad* (I, 2, 1), for instance, "the good (*śreyaḥ*) is one thing, the pleasant (*preyaḥ*) is another ... and he who chooses the pleasant falls from his true goal." The good is spiritual wisdom, self-knowledge; the pleasant is sensuous satisfaction or ego gratification: the good is the Real, the pleasant is the phenomenal.

All activities of the *jīva* who has not realized his true Self—whether they be mental (*mānasika*), verbal (*vācika*), or physical (*kāyika*) and no matter how noble or altruistic they may appear to be—suffer, according to Advaita, from the fact that they are rooted in a pleasure-seeking desire; consequently, unless transformed and redirected, they prevent one from attaining self-realization. Those activities of the self, then, that are so grounded in egoistic desire are bad, and those transformed and redirected activities that lead one to the good are good. Stated baldly and in somewhat different terms, as long as an act, desire, or thought leads one along the path of realization, it is, for Advaita Vedānta, morally justified. The end does justify the means—provided that the end is the highest value, the *summum bonum*, self-realization.[2] Apart from its general adherence to the traditional code of conduct, as this is limited and confined to the social order within the phenomenal world, this is the sole moral criterion proffered by the *Upaniṣads* as set forth in systematic Advaita.

The Advaitic aspirant, however, is not an ethical monster. Advaita does maintain, as we have seen in the analysis of *karma*,

2 In the *Bhagavadgītā*, for example, we find Arjuna (who is perhaps symbolic of one who is morally prepared to understand Vedānta) in the beginning being told all manner of simplicities in order to arouse him out of his passivity and lethargy: that he must fight in this just war, for otherwise his peers will think him cowardly (II, 34); that killing another person is not really killing him because he has to die sometime anyway (II, 18 and 27); and so on.

that although knowledge (*jñāna*) alone is sufficient to lead one to the highest goal or value, the cultivation of certain generally recognized virtues may be an aid to this attainment. The *Taittirīya Upaniṣad* (I, 2, 1) states that the disciple must "speak the truth (*satya*) and practice righteousness (*dharma*)." Moral virtues, such as compassion, charity, self-control, and non-injury, may be supports for the attainment of the spiritual end, although they are not the end themselves.[3]

But what about the man who has realized the highest value, who has gone beyond good and evil? Is he justified in committing any kind of act whatsoever? The logical answer to this is yes; but the psychological answer is no. According to Advaita, nothing that the realized person, the *jīvanmukta*, does is subject to moral judgment: he is no longer a judge himself, and he cannot be judged by a phenomenal scale of values. Psychologically, however, this does not mean that he could *in fact* perform certain actions that, from the lower standpoint, would be judged immoral (e.g., murder) because the performance of these actions presupposes egoism, a desire for self-enhancement and the like, on the part of the actor—an egoism that results from a false identification of the self with the body, senses, mind, and so forth. And if such egoism or ignorance were present, then the actor could not in fact be the realized sage.

The quality then that ought to inform human action is non-egoism which, positively expressed, is what the Advaitin understands to be "love." One must interrelate with "others," one must conduct onself, with the knowledge that the other is not-different from oneself. Love, the meeting of another in the depth of being, must be grounded in knowledge, and when it is so grounded, it expresses itself in every action that one performs.

3 Śaṁkara suggests in many places that the performance of good works may lead to rebirth in more advantageous forms and that it is a form of self-discipline, which is good training, as it were, for the more rigorous discipline of *jñāna-yoga*—the Advaitin's real path to knowledge and freedom.

8 Mokṣa and Jñāna-Yoga

I

The distinctive characteristic of most practical and theoretical concerns with freedom is the attempt to discover how one can be free *from* something: be it one's own passions and appetites, society, laws, or the forces of physical nature. Freedom is generally conceived of as that state of being or that opportunity which is on the other side of "necessity." Thomas Hobbes sums it up neatly when he writes that "liberty or freedom signifies properly the absence of opposition."[1]

The Advaitic concept of freedom (*mokṣa* or *mukti*) likewise is cast initially in negative terms, as freedom from *karma*, from actions that bind one to the world, and from the ceaseless round of births and deaths in the world (*saṁsāra*). But it also recognizes that when freedom is conceived of only in this negative sense of "freedom from," it is not something that human beings ultimately value; and that when taken to its fullest term, freedom is something from which they flee.

Whenever one is in a situation of strong constraint, one may indeed earnestly desire freedom from this constraint; one may even become obsessed with this desire to the point where one is rendered impotent to act effectively within the situation; but once all constraints are removed, one finds oneself facing an abyss. One doesn't know what to do, one doesn't know what to make of one's freedom, and rather than face an infinite possibility, one voluntarily seeks some other kind of constraint. We ceaselessly chain ourselves to things, to ideas, and to dreams and illusions. From some inner compulsion we turn away from the possibility of freedom. *We imitate the*

1 *The Leviathan*, II, 21.

servitude of others and convince ourselves that we are thereby fulfilling our social responsibility. "Freedom from" is denied by us. In human experience it turns out to be intolerably empty of substantial content.[2]

This "freedom from," however, does not exhaust the meaning of freedom: there is another kind of freedom that is a positive goal towards which men may strive. This other kind of freedom does not merely lie on the other side of constraint; rather all oppositions between "freedom from" and "necessity" are overcome by it.

The Sanskrit word *mokṣa* (or *mukti*) connotes to the Advaitin "freedom from *karma*" and also this other kind of spiritual freedom. *Mokṣa*, in the positive sense, means the attaining to a state of "at-one-ment" with the depth and quiescence of Reality and with the power of its creative becoming. Spiritual freedom means the full realization of the potentialities of man as a spiritual being. It means the attaining of insight into oneself; it means self-knowledge and joy of being.

II

Mokṣa or freedom is attained, according to Advaita Vedānta, through the mental-spiritual discipline of *jñāna-yoga*.[3] This dis-

2 This denigrating of "freedom from" is not meant, however, to deny the validity of the very important distinction between choosing one's own constraints and having them imposed upon one by others. The word "liberty" is perhaps most applicable here and is something that is indeed valuable. Because man is unable to endure "freedom from," in the full sense of the term, does not imply that he is then subject to whatever constraints may be imposed upon him. Self-chosen constraints are one thing, externally imposed constraints (or involuntary actions) are quite another thing.

3 The term "yoga" is probably derived from the root *yuj*, which means "to yoke," and has come to signify generally any path, way, or discipline that leads to spiritual experience. Many yogas are articulated in the Indian tradition. There is *karma-yoga*, the discipline of disinterested

cipline is a living process of knowing and being and cannot, therefore, in actuality be cut up into sharply delineated stages. Nevertheless, for the purpose of instruction, Advaita does set forth as a model or ideal schema a set of four general qualifications that must be fulfilled by the person who would attain *mokṣa* and three general stages that he must traverse.

The four qualifications are:[4]

1. That the aspirant must possess the native ability to discern between what is real and what is only apparently real, between truth that is timeless and events that are time-bound. He must, in short, have the ability to discriminate (*viveka*) between the spiritual and the superficial.

2. That he must have an utter disregard for those sensuous pleasures that distract the mind. He must willfully and joyfully give up everything that stands in the way to the attainment of truth and self-knowledge. This second qualification demands the renunciation of, or indifference to (*vairāgya*), all petty desires, to all strivings for sensuous self-satisfaction.

3. That he must acquire mental tranquility (*sama*), self-control (*dama*), dispassion (*uparati*), endurance (*titikṣā*), intentness of mind (*samādhāna*), and faith (*śraddhā*).

4. That he must have a positive longing for freedom and wisdom (*mumukṣutva*). He must dedicate himself completely to the quest for understanding, concentrating all desire upon it alone.

action that is emphasized in the *Bhagavadgītā*; *rāja-yoga*, the ancient "psychological" path codified by Patañjali; *bhakti-yoga*, the way of love or devotion that is prevalent among the various sects of Vaiṣṇavism and Śaivism; and *jñāna-yoga*, the discipline of knowledge that is associated with Advaita Vedānta. Although tradition has it that all yogas, when earnestly pursued, lead to the same end, namely, *mokṣa*, Indian philosophy generally believes that there is a hierarchy among them with respect to their difficulty and to the ends achieved. *Jñāna-yoga* is taken by the Advaitin as the most difficult discipline and as the one that yields the fullest possible spiritual experience.

4 Cf. Śaṁkara, *Brahmasūtrabhāṣya*, I, 1, 1.

This *sādhana catuṣṭaya*, or fourfold discipline, of Vedānta is clearly not one that any merely rational person can follow. It requires a radical change in the natural direction of consciousness that leads one to a passionate involvement with the things of the world. Advaita Vedānta is explicitly aristocratic in its contention that, practically speaking, truth or genuine knowledge is available only to the few who, by natural temperament and disposition, are willing and able to undertake all the arduous demands that its quest entails.

Once the aspirant has indicated his capacity and his will to attain *mokṣa*, he embarks upon the three general stages of *jñāna-yoga* proper.

"Hearing" (*śravaṇa*), the first of the three, has to do with the initial (and sometimes immediately enlightening) acquaintance with the teachings of Advaita. The aspirant is encouraged to listen to the sages and to study the Vedāntic texts. He must investigate the *mahāvākyas* or "great sayings" of the Upaniṣads and determine their proper purport. The listening and studying orient the mind to what is to be sought and provide a framework, grounded in other's experience, by means of which the aspirant's own subsequent experience can be interpreted and made commensurate with the tradition.

Since medieval times we in the West have been wanting in this kind of traditional orientation and interpretation, and although this lack has provided us with the opportunity for fresh and creative approaches to many areas of experience, it also has made it very difficult for us to sustain our spiritual experience and integrate it with the rest of our life. In our culture we are each called upon to work out an individual justification (philosophical and other) both for the quest of self-knowledge and for whatever results are obtained. A tradition can eliminate this individual need and thereby give the individual the opportunity to strengthen and deepen his development. Rather than having to spend the time and energy to work out intellectually all the philosophical answers for himself, he can continue along his way and devote all of his energies to it. A tradition can, to be sure, stultify experience (by demanding that all experience conform to it), and it can make it somewhat too easy to have the answers (with worn-out jargon being a substitute for real insight and understanding). Advaita Vedānta does believe, however—and perhaps rightly so?—that the advantages of tradition outweigh the disadvantages.

Still one must not see the traditional element in the Advaitin's yoga in too narrow a manner. For in the second stage, which is that of "thinking" (designated in Sanskrit usually as *manana*), the Advaitic seeker is called upon to appropriate inwardly, by means of prolonged reflection, the philosophical principles of Advaita and make these the stuff of his own living faith. He is to see for himself the rightness of these principles and, although at this point they are only abstractions, he becomes convinced of their validity. Through the help of a *guru* or "master," the aspirant learns about the nature of Brahman, of its definition as *saccidānanda*, being, consciousness, and bliss, of the philosophical basis for the *via negativa* by which it is obtained, and of the distinction between *nirguṇa* and *saguṇa* Brahman, Brahman without, and with, qualities. He is taught the proper discrimination between the levels of being and the manner in which these levels are constituted by experience. The fundamental distinction between Reality and Appearance is driven home to him by a careful analysis of his experience in terms of *māyā*, *avidyā*, and *adhyāsa*. He comes to understand why he ascribes independent reality to the contents of his experience and how his ego and desires determine the quality of his experience. He is forced to look within and see for himself the manner in which he erroneously identifies himself with some phenomenal or partial expression of his self. The levels of selfhood, as revealed by the degrees of consciousness that he recognizes and by their respective contents, is analyzed, and the basic distinction between *Ātman* and *jīva* is made manifest to him. He explores the workings of knowledge, of the *pramāṇas*, and recognizes how his knowledge of the world is constituted and what its conditions are. He grounds himself thoroughly in the values that inform his quest, understanding the supreme value of freedom towards which he strives.

"The self that I ordinarily see," says the aspirant, "—this is not Me; the world as it presents itself to me with its divisions and contradictions, this cannot be Real. With intellect alone, I remain outside of everything. I ask something in Nature what it is and receive as an answer only my own categories and classifications. Led from one thing to another, I do not grasp what *is*. 'Who are you?'—I might silently ask another, and as soon as I make noise within myself, I fail to find the answer. Desires, needs, attachments well up within me and bind me to what I should not be.

"What is the body? What is the mind? Am I only a collection of the accidents of birth, of language, of country? I am awake, I dream, and sometimes I seem to rest peacefully in my very being. The body changes and deteriorates. *It cannot be the Self.* The mind is fickle, intemperate, and yet powerful. It enables me to master my environment—but what does this mastery mean? Today I am a success, tomorrow, a failure. Should I be only the praise and blame of others? Civilizations come and go; what meaning, then, can my petty mastery have? Awake, I am the world: it and me are so mutually involved that I can only partially discriminate between them. Asleep, I still remain its victim. And even when awake, am I not still half-asleep? I cannot completely control the stream of images, of desires, of memories—of nonsense—that is so much a part of my waking consciousness. *The mind cannot be the Self.* Still there are moments of intense well-being; of self-satisfaction and aesthetic delight. Unself-consciously I find myself to be a part of something else; I give myself over to it and find a wonderful harmony there. Everything finds its place here. Without fear, without anxiety, without restlessness and ambition, and without the need to possess, I realize the immense potentiality of being, the power that sustains life. But this state of being too is transitory. *This feeling and knowing self, this state of delightful harmony cannot be the Self.*

"Events appear and disappear. I accept some and reject others. What is important to me today, I discover to be unimportant to me tomorrow. Truths are turned into illusions: what I value most before attaining it, I disvalue when I attain it. The things of the world—power, prestige, money, even family and home—turn out to be empty: instead of liberating they bind me. Everything gets rejected by something else. No *thing*, then, can be truly real.

"The more I learn, the less I know what is of real value to me. The more I strive, the less I know where I am going. Around and around I am turned. What do I really know? I see the world in terms of my knowledge and desire, and therefore I do not really see the world at all. This world of mine cannot be Real."

The actual experiential attainment of *mokṣa*, of self-knowledge and wisdom, for most Advaitins, is the work of the third stage which is that of "constant meditation" (*nididhyāsana*). If the disciple has been successful in his reflection, he is then ready to strive for direct self-realization. He must meditate, he must maintain an intense concentration on the identity of his self with Reality. Dissociating himself from the phenomenal play of his surface life, he must become a witness to it. Through detachment he turns away from all egoism, from all fear and sense-distraction. He discriminates away all that stands in the way of the Self. *Neti neti*, the Self is not this, not this: "my," "me," "mine" become sounds signifying nothing. *Tat tvam asi*—the Self is Reality. "You" and "me" are not-different. Causes and effects are mutually involved: the material elements (gross and subtle) that constitute physical nature are ontologically nothing but their cause, namely, *ahaṁkāra* (I-consciousness) and *buddhi* (intelligence); they are nothing but their cause, namely, *saguṇa* Brahman, or consciousness associated with *māyā*, and *saguṇa* Brahman has its ultimate ground in pure consciousness or *nirguṇa* Brahman. Desuperimposition (*apavāda*), the reducing of effects back into their causes, the discriminating away of all lower levels of experience, is the sword that cuts away false identifications. It culminates in those "great sayings," *ahaṁ brahmāsi*—I am Brahman, there are no distinctions in Reality—and *tat tvam asi*—thou art that; Brahman is one and all is Brahman.[5]

To the *jīvanmukta*, to the man who is free while living, Brahman is everywhere seen. *Mokṣa* or *mukti*, freedom or liberation, as realized through *jñāna-yoga*, is just this power of being and seeing that excludes nothing, that includes everything. Brahman is One. Everything has its being in Spirit: everything, in its true being, is Brahman.

5 In post-Śaṁkara Advaita several different interpretations of the "Three stages" (and the relations between them) are given. The *Vivaraṇa* school generally holds to the view that it is only through the mediation of the *mahāvākyas* that the self may be apprehended. It thereby emphasizes *śravaṇa* and places *manana* and *nididhyāsana* in subordinate roles. For purposes of a reconstruction, however, we can better follow those Advaitins like Maṇḍana and Vācaspati who look to intellectual discrimination and meditation as the most efficacious means to *mokṣa*.

Bibliography

RECOMMENDED GENERAL WORKS ON INDIAN PHILOSOPHY

Chatterjee, Satischandra, and Datta, Dhirendramohan. *An Introduction to Indian Philosophy*. Calcutta: University of Calcutta, 1960.

Dasgupta, Surendranath. *A History of Indian Philosophy*. 5 vols. Cambridge: Cambridge University Press, 1922–55.

———. *Indian Idealism*. Cambridge: Cambridge University Press, 1933.

Hiriyanna, Mysore. *The Essentials of Indian Philosophy*. London: George Allen & Unwin, 1932.

———. *Outlines of Indian Philosophy*. London: George Allen & Unwin, 1932.

Moore, Charles A. (ed.). *The Indian Mind*. Honolulu: East-West Center Press and University of Hawaii Press, 1967.

Potter, Karl. *Presuppositions of India's Philosophies*. Englewood Cliffs, New Jersey: Prentice-Hall, Inc., 1963.

Radhakrishnan, Sarvepalli. *Indian Philosophy*. 2 vols. London: George Allen & Unwin, 1923, 1927.

Sharma, Chandradhar. *Indian Philosophy: A Critical Survey*. New York: Barnes & Noble, Inc., 1962.

Smart, Ninian. *Doctrine and Argument in Indian Philosophy*. London: George Allen & Unwin, 1964.

Zimmer, Heinrich. *Philosophies of India*. Edited by Joseph Campbell. London: Routledge and Kegan Paul, 1952.

SOME PRIMARY SOURCES IN ADVAITA VEDĀNTA IN ENGLISH TRANSLATION

Alston, A. J., trans. *The Naiṣkarmya Siddhi of Śrī Sureśvara*. London: Shanti Sadan, 1959.

Apte, V. M., trans. *Brahma-Sūtra-Shankara-Bhāshya*. Bombay: Popular Book Depot, 1960.

Bhattacharyya, Vidhushekhara, ed. and trans. *The Āgamaśāstra of Gauḍapāda*. Calcutta: University of Calcutta, 1943.

Chatterjee, Mohini M., trans. *Viveka-cūḍāmaṇi, or Crest-Jewel of Wisdom of Śrī Śaṁkarācārya*. Adyar: Theosophical Publishing House, 1947.

Date, Vinayak Hari, trans. *Vedānta Explained, Śaṁkara's Commentary on the Brahma-sūtras.* 2 vols. Bombay: Bookseller's Publishing Co., 1954.

Devanji, Prahlad Chandrashekha, trans. *Siddhantabindu by Madhusūdanasarasvati: A Commentary on the Daśaśloki of Śaṁkarācārya.* ("Gaekwad's Oriental Series," Vol. LXIV.) Baroda: Oriental Institute, 1933.

Hiriyanna, Mysore, ed. and trans. *Vedānta-sāra (by Sadānanda): A Work on Vedānta Philosophy.* Poona: Oriental Book Agency, 1929.

Jagadānanda, Swāmi, trans. *Upadeshasāhasrī of Srī Sankarāchārya* ("A Thousand Teachings"). Mylapore, Madras: Sri Ramakrishna Math, 1961.

Jha, Ganganatha, trans. *The Chāndogyaopaniṣad* ("A Treatise on Vedānta Philosophy Translated into English with the Commentary of Śankara"). Poona: Oriental Book Agency, 1942.

Kamarkar, Raghunath Damodar, ed. and trans. *Gauḍapāda-Kārikā.* Poona: Bhandarkar Oriental Research Institute, 1953.

———, ed. and trans. *Vedāntakalpalatikā by Madhusūdana Sarvastī.* Poona: Bhandarkar Oriental Research Institute, 1962.

Madhavananda, Swāmī, trans. *The Bṛhadāraṇyaka Upaniṣad: with the Commentary of Śankarācārya.* Mayavati, Almora, Himalayas: Advaita Ashrama, 1950.

Mahadevan, T. M. P., ed. and trans. *The Saṁbandha-Vārtika of Sureśvarācārya.* Madras: University of Madras, 1958.

Nikhilanānda, Swāmī, trans. *The Māṇḍūkhyopaniṣad with Gauḍapāda's Kārikā and Śaṅkara's Commentary.* Mysore: Sri Ramakrishnan Asrama, 1955.

———, trans. *Self-Knowledge: An English Translation of Śaṅkarāchārya's Ātmabodha.* Mylapore, Madras: Sri Ramakrishna Math, 1947.

———, trans. *Vedantasara: or The Essence of Vedanta of Sadananda Yogindra.* Mayavati, Almora, Himalayas: Advaita Ashrama, 1949.

Śāstrī, S. Subrahmaṇya, and Ayyaṅgār, T. R. Śrīnivāsa, ed. and trans. *The Jīvan-Mukti-Viveka* ("The Path to Liberation-In-This-Life of Śrī Vidyāraṇya)." Madras: The Theosophical Publishing House, n.d.

Sastri, S. S. Suryanarayana, trans. *Siddhanta-leśa-saṅgraha.* Madras: University of Madras, 1935.

———, ed. and trans. *Vedāntaparibhāṣā by Dhamarāja Ahdvarin*: Adyar: The Adyar Library, 1942.

Sastri, S. S. Suryanarayana, and Raja, C. Kunhan, ed. and trans. *The Bhāmatī of Vācaspati: on Śaṅkara's Brahmasutrabhāṣya (Catussūtrī)*. Madras: Theosophical Publishing House, 1933.

Sastri, S. S. Suryanarayana, and Sen, Saileswar, trans. *Vivaraṇa-prameya-saṅgraha*. Madras: The Sri Vidya Press, 1941.

Sastry, A. Mahadeva, trans. *The Bhagavad-Gita: with the Commentary of Sri Sankaracharya*. Madras: V.Ramaswamy Sastrulu & Sons, 1961.

Shastri, Hari Prasad, trans. *Panchadasi: A Treatise on Advaita Metaphysics by Swami Vidyaranya*. London: Shanti Sadan, 1956.

Thibaut, George, trans. *The Vedānta-sūtras with the Commentary of Śaṅkarācārya*. Vols. XXXIV and XXXVIII of *Sacred Books of the East*. Edited by Max Müller. Oxford: The Clarendon Press, 1890 and 1896.

Venkararamiah, D., trans. *The Pañcapādika of Padmapāda* ("Gaekwad's Oriental Series," Vol. CVII). Baroda: Oriental Institute, 1948.

SOME SECONDARY SOURCES ON ADVAITA VEDĀNTA

Belvalkar, S. K. *Vedānta Philosophy*. Poona: Bilrakunja Publishing House, 1929.

Bhattacharya, Asutosh Sastri. *Studies in Post-Śaṇkara Dialectics*. Calcutta: University of Calcutta, 1936.

Bhattacharyya, K. C. *Studies in Vedāntism*. Calcutta: University of Calcutta, 1909.

Bhattacharyya, Kokileswar. *An Introduction to Adwaita Philosophy*. Calcutta: University of Calcutta, 1924.

Chaudhuri, Amil Kumar Ray. *Self and Falsity in Advaita Vedānta*. Calcutta: Progressive Publishers, 1955.

Das, Saroj Kumar. *A Study of the Vedānta*. Calcutta: University of Calcutta, 1937.

Datta, Dhirendra Mohan. "Inward and Outward Advaita Vedānta," *The Philosophical Quarterly*, Vol. XXX (October, 1957), pp. 165–72.

———. *The Six Ways of Knowing: A Critical Study of the Vedānta Theory of Knowledge*. 2nd rev. ed. Calcutta: The University of Calcutta, 1960.

Devaraja, N. K. *An Introduction to Śaṅkara's Theory of Knowledge*. Delhi: Motilal Banarsi Dass, 1962.

Guénon, René. *Man and His Becoming According to the Vedānta.* Translated by Richard C. Nicholson. New York: The Noonday Press, 1958.

Hacker, Paul. *Vivarta: Studien zur Geschichte der illustionistischen Kasmologie und Erkenntnistheorie der Inder.* Wiesbaden: Akademie der Wissenschaften und der Litteratur in Mainz, 1953.

Hasurkar, S. S. *Vācaspati Miśra on Advaita Vedānta.* Darbhanga: Mithila Institute, 1958.

Ingalls, Daniel H. H. "Śaṃkara on the Question: Whose Avidya?" *Philosophy East and West,* III, No. 1, 69–72 (1953).

———. "Śaṃkara's Arguments against the Buddhists," *Philosophy East and West,* III, No. 4, 291–306 (1954).

Iyer, K. A. Krishnaswami. *Vedanta, or the Science of Reality.* Madras: Ganesh and Co., 1930.

Lacombe, Olivier. *L'Absolu selon le Vedānta.* Paris: P. Geuthner, 1937.

Levy, John. *The Nature of Man According to the Vedanta.* London: Routledge and Kegan Paul, 1956.

Mahadevan, T. M. P. *The Philosophy of Advaita.* London: Luzac and Co., 1938.

———. *Gauḍapāda: A Study in Early Advaita.* Madras: University of Madras, 1954.

Malkani, G. R. *Vedantic Epistemology.* Amalner: The Indian Institute of Philosophy, 1953.

Murty, K. Satchidananda. *Revelation and Reason in Advaita Vedānta.* New York: Columbia University Press, 1961.

Sastri, Kokileswar. *An Introduction to Advaita Philosophy.* Calcutta: University of Calcutta, 1926.

SenGupta, B. K. *A Critique on the Vivaraṇa School.* Calcutta: The Author, 1959.

Singh, Ram Pratap. *The Vedānta of Śaṅkara—A Metaphysics of Value.* Vol. I Jaipur: Bharat Publishing House, 1949.

Sircar, Mahendranath. *Comparative Studies in Vedantism.* Bombay: Humphrey Milford, 1927.

Staal, J. F. *Advaita and Neo-Platonism: A Critical Study in Comparative Philosophy.* Madras: University of Madras, 1961.

Upadhyaya, Veermani Prasad. *Lights on Vedānta.* ("Chowkhamba Sanskrit Series," Vol. VI.) Varanasi, 1959.

Urguhart, W. S. *The Vedanta and Modern Thought.* London: Oxford University Press, 1928.

Index

modes of 12; experience of, 29; role of positive characterization of, 11, 13; as object of knowledge, 84. See also *nirguṇa* Brahman; *saguṇa* Brahman
Brahma-sūtras, 3. *See also* Śaṁkara
Brāhmaṇas, 9
Bṛhad-āraṇyaka Upaniṣad, 5n*4*, 11, 27n*3*, 48n*2*, 57n*19*. *See also* Śaṁkara
buddhi (intellect), 59
Buddhism, 6, 35n*16*

causation. See *satkāryavāda*; *vivartavādā*; *pariṇāmavāda*
Chāndogya Upaniṣad, 5n*4*, 27n*3*, 49n*8*
cit (consciousness), 9, 10
consciousness: as symbol of Brahman, 10; pure consciousness of Ātman, 48, 49; states of, 55–64 *passim*; continuity of, 57. See also *cit*
creation, 27, 30, 39, 40. See also *līlā*

Datta, D. M. 74n*14*
dharma (righteousness), 100, 102
Dharmarāja, 4n*2*, 73
doubt, 60, 88, 89
dṛṣṭisṛṣṭivāda (perception is creation), 31n*8*

Eliot, Charles, 68n*4*
epistemology, 29, 81–97 *passim*, 99. See also *pramāṇas*
ethics, 99–102
existent, 21

falsity, 87, 90, 92
freedom. See *mokṣa*
Freud, Sigmund, 59

Gauḍapāda, 4n*2*
Geldner, Karl Friedrich, 68n*4*

hetu (reason on basis of inference), 71
heuristic principle, 43, 92
Hiriyanna, M., 67n*3*
Hobbes, Thomas, 103

ignorance. See *avidyā*
illusory existent, 23, 25, 25n*8*
immortality, 48, 59
indriyas (senses), 70. *See also* senses
Īśā Upaniṣad, 5n*4*
Īśvara (personal God), 12n*7*, 28, 38, 39, 43, 63

jāgarita-sthāna (waking consciousness), 55
Jainism, 6
jīva (empirical self): status of, 51; states of consciousness of, 55–65 *passim*; and *karma*, 67; freedom of, 58
jīvanmukta (free while living), 76n*18*, 102, 110
jñāna (knowledge, insight), 13, 30
jñāna-yoga, 100n*1*, 102n*3*, 103–110 *passim*

judgment: error of, 16; revision of, 16; validity of, 86–90 *passim*; support for, 88

kāraṇa-śarīra (causal body), 61
karma: definition of, 67; relation to *saṁsāra*, 67n*3*; origin of idea, 68n*4*; status of (as "convenient fiction"), 69–76 *passim*; kinds of, 76n*18*
karma-yoga, 104n*3*
Kaṭha Upaniṣad, 27n*5*, 48n*3*, 77n*21*, 100, 101. *See also* Śaṁkara
Keith, A. Berriedale, 27n*4*, 68n*4*
Kena Upaniṣad, 27n*5*, 49n*5*
knowledge: means of, 69–75 *passim*; 83, 90; validity of, 86–90 *passim*. See also *vidyā*; *parāvidyā*; *jñāna*
Kumārila, 86

Lacombe, Olivier, 39n*23*
levels of being, 25, 25n*9*, 29, 44
liberty, 104n*2*
līlā (sport), 38–41
logical relations, 21, 22
love, 13, 20, 102. See also *bhakti*

Macdonnell, A. A., 68n*4*
Madhva, 3
mahāvākya (great saying), 49, 106
manana (thinking), 107, 110n*5*
manas(sense-mind), 27n*4*, 59, 70, 91
Maṇḍana, 3n*2*, 31n*7*, 110n*5*
Māṇḍūkya Upaniṣad, 55–62
manomayakośa (sheath of mind), 58–59
māyā (illusion): definition of, 28–34 *passim*; Vedic usage, 30; relation to *avidyā*, 30, 33; concealing and distorting powers, 30–31; creative power of, 30; justification for, 42
Mīmāṁsā, 35n*16*, 69, 86
mind. See *manas; buddhi*
mithyā (false), 54
mokṣa (freedom), 75, 76, 79, 103–110 *passim*
morality, 77, 100. *See also* ethics
mukti. See *mokṣa*
Muṇḍaka Upaniṣad, 27n*1*, 49n*6*, 81, 84n*4*, 100

nāma-rūpa (name and form), 38, 73, 95
neti neti, 11, 109
nididhyāsana (constant meditation), 109, 110n*5*
nirguṇa Brahman (Brahman without qualities), 12, 13, 14, 107. *See also* Brahman; *saguṇa* Brahman
nirvikalpa samādhi (indeterminate experience), 13, 62–63
non-dualism, 3
null class, 92
Nyāya, 6, 35n*16*, 69, 87, 93n*12*

ontology, 15, 99

Padmapāda, 3n*2*, 13n*2*
paramātman (highest self), 48
paramārthika, 26n*10*
parāvidyā (higher knowledge), 81, 82, 85, 99